USEFUL PHRASES
TRAVEL TIPS
ETIQUETTE

JAPANESE
FOR TRAVELERS

THE INDISPENSABLE GUIDE TO JAPAN

S0-AFN-073

Scott Rutherford

TUTTLE PUBLISHING
Tokyo • Rutland, Vermont • Singapore

Published by Tuttle Publishing, an imprint of Periplus Editions (HK) Ltd., with editorial offices at 364 Innovation Drive, North Clarendon, Vermont 05759 U.S.A.

Library of Congress Cataloging-in-Publication Data

Rutherford, Scott.
  Japanese for travelers : useful phrases, travel tips, & etiquette / by Scott Rutherford.
    p. cm.
  ISBN 978-4-8053-1046-5 (pbk.)
1. Japanese language--Conversation and phrase books--English. I. Title.
PL539.R87 2009
495.6'83421--dc22

                           2008038714

ISBN 978-4-8053-1046-5

Distributed by

North America, Latin America & Europe	**Japan**	**Asia Pacific**
Tuttle Publishing	Tuttle Publishing	Berkeley Books Pte. Ltd.
364 Innovation Drive	Yaekari Building, 3rd Floor	61 Tai Seng Avenue #02-12
North Clarendon,	5-4-12 Osaki	Singapore 534167
VT 05759-9436 U.S.A.	Shinagawa-ku	Tel: (65) 6280-1330
Tel: 1 (802) 773-8930	Tokyo 141 0032	Fax: (65) 6280-6290
Fax: 1 (802) 773-6993	Tel: (81) 03 5437-0171	inquiries@periplus.com.sg
info@tuttlepublishing.com	Fax: (81) 03 5437-0755	www.periplus.com
www.tuttlepublishing.com	tuttle-sales@gol.com	

First edition
13 12 11 10 09   10 9 8 7 6 5 4 3 2 1

Printed in Singapore

TUTTLE PUBLISHING® is a registered trademark of Tuttle Publishing, a division of Periplus Editions (HK) Ltd.

Contents

Basics

BASICS

Basics
GRAMMAR

文法

bunpō
grammar

There's no way to become fluent in Japanese in a week, three weeks, or three months. Probably not in a year, or even three. Certainly not by using this book, for it's not intended to be a language course.

Spoken Japanese is not especially difficult: neither grammar nor syntax is particularly complex. In fact, Japanese is probably easier to learn than English. (The Japanese, however, prefer perpetuating the myth that Japanese is the world's most difficult language.)

Written Japanese, on the other hand, is a challenge. It uses *katakana* and *hiragana*—two phonetic alphabets—and around 2,000 Chinese characters, or *kanji*. Roman letters also often appear, especially in advertising.

Most difficult, however, are the embedded cultural and social codes of the Japanese language. To fully grasp the more veiled of these practically requires being born Japanese.

Within a group, the ideal form of communication is that which is sparse and ambiguous. Messages are conveyed through verbal fuzziness, contextual clarity, and implication. This semi-verbal mode of communication is called *ishin denshin*, or "telepathic" communication. Different as it is from the directness preferred by many Westerners, it plays an important role in reinforcing Japanese feelings of uniqueness.

ORIENTATION

For many Japanese, their language is a cocoon that defines the group, the nation, and the race. Recognizing you as a foreigner, Japanese will often operate on the assumption that you most certainly can't understand their language. This assumption is so strong that even when a foreigner speaks their language well, Japanese people sometimes do not seem to realize that their language is being spoken. Some people may talk about you openly in the elevator or in stores, especially outside the major cities. Mothers have been heard telling children in restaurants to "watch how the foreigner eats," especially if the foreigner is using chopsticks. You are, you will learn quickly, a thing of curiosity, especially outside of Tokyo and Osaka.

On the other hand, being a curiosity can have its advantages. Whatever mistake or gaffe you make, you're an outsider and a foreigner, and your mistakes are generally dismissed on that basis. You're not Japanese, after all.

Here are some terms related to Japanese language and grammar:

WORD 単語 tango	GRAMMAR 文法 bunpō	DIALECT 方言 hōgen	CHINESE CHARACTER 漢字 kanji
SENTENCE 文 bun	MEANING 意味 imi	QUESTION 質問 shitsumon	ROMAN LETTERS ローマ字 Rōmaji
HORIZONTAL WRITING 横書き yokogaki	PRONUNCIATION 発音 hatsuon	FOREIGN LANGUAGE 外国語 gaikokugo	HIRAGANA ひらがな hiragana
VERTICAL WRITING 縦書き tategaki	ACCENT アクセント akusento	CHARACTER, LETTER 字、文字 ji, moji	KATAKANA カタカナ katakana

JAPANESE 日本語 nihongo	ENGLISH 英語 eigo	CONVERSATION 会話 kaiwa	WORD, LANGUAGE 言葉 kotoba

PRONUNCIATION

Japanese sounds like all mush unless one takes care with the pronunciation of vowels. English-speakers typically utter sloppy-sounding vowels, making a muck of languages, like Spanish and Japanese, that require precision in vowel sounds. A native English-speaker's thick accent is often the result of laziness in vowel pronunciation.

It's this simple: if you want to be understood when you speak, be diligent in pronunciation.

Vowels

In short, each Japanese **vowel** has a single sound, as spoken in the following words:

   a   as in father
   i   as in sushi
   u   as in rude
   e   as in egg
   o   as in oat

Sometimes, Japanese vowels are pronounced in 2 beats, instead of one. For example, the word *sōji*, or "cleaning," is pronounced *so'oji*. This book follows standard convention by using macrons (lines) over all double vowels except *i*. The double *i* sound is represented as *ii*. It is important to be aware of this nuance of pronunciation, as the length of a vowel can change the meaning of a word completely. For example, *hodō* means "sidewalk," but *hōdō* means "news report."

In regular Japanese conversation, the *i* and *u* sounds are often not heard at all. For example, the name Matsushita becomes Matsush'ta, and *kusuri*, meaning "medicine," becomes *k'suri*. De-emphasis of *i* and *u* is especially common after the *sh* and *k* sounds.

Consonants

Japanese **consonants** are generally similar to English ones, but there are some important differences.

F

The Japanese ear doesn't distinguish between the English *f* and *h* sounds. (On some maps of Japan rendered into English by

Japanese speakers, Mt. Fuji may be written as "Mt. Huji.")

The Japanese *f* is not a strong *f* sound, but is halfway between the English *f* and *h*, like an *f* sound in which the upper teeth do not meet the lower lip, and air is forced out through narrowed lips.

G

Always *g*, as in "gate." Often softened into *ng*, as in "sing."

R

The Japanese inability to distinguish between the English *r* and *l* is often a mother lode of snickers—"rice" becomes "lice" in a restaurant, "election" becomes "erection" at cocktail parties. The Japanese *r* hovers somewhere between the English *r* and *l*. As with the English *l*, the tongue is placed on the ridge behind the upper teeth, but with a lighter touch.

Like vowels, consonants are sometimes pronounced in two beats. Again, this is a crucial distinction, because a word's meaning can utterly change as the result of just a single doubled sound. Doubling is especially common for *t*, *p*, and *k*. This book expresses doubled consonants as double letters: *tt*, *pp*, *kk*, etc.

Unlike English, in which every multisyllabic word stresses a particular syllable, Japanese does not stress syllables at all. For instance, although the Japanese word for banana is very similar to the English, the pronunciation is considerably different. The Japanese word is pronounced *ba-na-na*, with each *a* sounding like the *a* in "father," and each syllable having equal intensity.

While stress is not important, however, proper pitch is very important. A word's dictionary meaning doesn't change with pitch, but the unspoken message and mood can, and usually do.

Japanese language books commonly explain that the subject of a sentence is marked by *wa*, or in certain cases, *ga*. This is not, in fact, always the case. But, for our minimal needs, we'll simplify life by designating *wa-* and *ga-* marked words as subjects.

Mearii wa (kaerimashita).
Mary (went home).

Note that there is no difference in Japanese between singular and plural subjects. Like much in the language, they are inferred from context.

SENTENCE SUBJECT

Unlike in English, the subject or focus of the sentence in Japanese is often unspoken, implied instead through context. In fact, using the subject sometimes overemphasizes it, flooding it with spotlights and exclamation points. This is a pitfall for foreigners learning Japanese, who try to put in subjects at every pause. This tendency is automatic, but produces an undesirable effect. In the examples below, the subjects "I" and "flower" are left unsaid.

I am Mary.	The flower was pretty.
(Watashi wa) Mearii desu.	*(Hana wa) Kirei deshita.*
(I) Mary am.	(Flower) Pretty was.

Even though the speaker may not state the subject explicitly, it should be clear; context remedies ambiguity. It is a deeply embedded Japanese cultural and linguistic trait to prefer saying and explaining as little as possible. Proficiency in Japanese requires substantial patience and intuition for the unsaid. Think of Japanese as a minimalist language, in company with traditional Japanese design and aesthetics.

this	kore	これ	**I**	watashi	私
that	sore	それ	**we**	watashitachi	私たち
that	are	あれ	**you** (sng.)	anata	あなた
this ~	kono ~	この〜	**you** (plural)	anatagata	あなたがた
that ~	sono ~	その〜	**HE**	kare	彼
that ~	ano ~	あの〜	**she**	kanojo	彼女

Japanese people often prefer to avoid direct and explicit requests. Instead, requests are understood from context and intonation.

Indirectness is a social tool to maintain harmony and avoid direct confrontation. Regardless of the realities of a situation, a request is best phrased and spoken in a way that enables the listener to appear to grant the favor through his own will. Westerners may think it's like a game, this diplomatic finessing of words and meaning—but it works for the Japanese.

As is the case with many languages, perfect and complete sentences are often not normal in conversational Japanese. When offering a cold beer in English, one needn't say, "Please have this cold beer." Rather, one might hold out the beer and simply say, "Please." And so in Japanese, too, one can offer something by simply saying *dōzo*. A complete sentence, in fact, would sound stuffy and artificial.

A request usually ends with *kudasai*, roughly translated as "Please." For instance:

Please be quiet.	A beer, please.
Shizuka ni shite kudasai.	*Biiru o kudasai.*

On the other hand, if someone offers you something, then you should reply *onegai shimasu*, which can be thought of as "Yes, please."

Would you like some coffee?	Yes, please.
Kōhii wa ikaga desu ka?	*Hai, onegai shimasu.*

To make things simple, stick to these guidelines: (1) When offering something, say *dōzo*; (2) When requesting something, use *kudasai*; and (3) When accepting an offer, use *onegai shimasu*.

VERBS

While this book isn't a grammar text, it will be worth your while to understand the basic verb forms used here. Besides, Japanese verbs conjugate consistently and straightforwardly; they're a piece of cake.

The infinitive (basic) form of all verbs ends with an *u* sound. Aside from being the "main" form of verbs (the one, for instance, that you'd look for in a dictionary), this is also the informal form, the one used with family and friends. In more polite language, such as that used with strangers on the street or casual acquaintances, the infinitive verb is changed so that it ends in *-masu*. Verbs that end with *u* or *-masu* can be used to indicate either the present or the future tense.

Verbs are classified based on their endings and are conjugated

13

into their *-masu* form and other forms accordingly. A simple overview of endings and their conjugations appears on page 15.

Let's look at a couple of verbs in use. *Aru* means "to exist," and is used only for inanimate objects.

There is a book.	There was a book.
Hon ga aru. (informal)	*Hon ga atta.* (informal)
Hon ga arimasu. (polite)	*Hon ga arimashita.* (polite)

For animate objects like animals and people, *iru* is used.

There is a person.	There was a person.
Hito ga iru. (informal)	*Hito ga ita.* (informal)
Hito ga imasu. (polite)	*Hito ga imashita.* (polite)

The common word *desu*, which loosely translates as "is," is like a verb, but is technically considered a different animal, The polite past tense of *desu* is *deshita*. Desu is used with both animate and inanimate things, and is remarkably useful.

I am Mary. (My name is Mary)	It's a desk.
Mearii desu.	*Tsukue desu.*
I am an American.	He was a teacher.
Amerikajin desu.	*Sensei deshita.*

VERB (Non-past, infinitive)	Ending Type	Polite Non-past	Informal Past	Polite Past
TABERU (to eat)	-eru	Tabemasu	Tabeta	Tabemasbita
DEKIRU (to do)	-iru	Dekimasu	Dekita	Dekimashita
AU (to meet)	-au	Aimasu	Atta	Aimashita
IKU (to go)	-ku	Ikimasu	Itta	Ikimashita
HANASU (to speak)	-su	Hanashimasu	Hanashita	Hanashimashita
MATSU (to wait)	-tsu	Machimasu	Matta	Machimashita
ASOBU (to play)	-bu	Asobimasu	Asonda	Asobimashita
YOMU (to read)	-mu	Yomimasu	Yonda	Yomimashita
SUWARU (to sit)	-ru	Suwarimasu	Suwatta	Suwarimashita

ESSENTIAL VERBS

to be able to hear
聞こえる
kikoeru

to ask a question
質問する
shitsumon suru

to talk, speak
話す
hanasu

to hear, ask
聞く
kiku

to pronounce
発音する
hatsuon suru

to read
読む
yomu

to listen
聴く
kiku

to say, tell
言う
iu

to write
書く
kaku

QUESTIONS

An important difference distinguishing declarative sentences from questions is a marker often nailed onto the end of the latter: *ka?* Listen for it. If someone deluges you with Japanese that you find quite incomprehensible, and the final sound is *ka*, a response is expected. Any response. Even a response of not understanding. Figure out from context if a simple yes or no is required, or turn to the bottom of page 55 and point to the appropriate expression, making it clear that nothing's registering.

A related marker, though not exactly one indicating a question, is *ne*. *Ne* comes after an assertion to soften it and could be thought of as "... isn't it?" or "... don't you think?" Let's compare some examples.

It's hot today.
Kyō wa atsui desu.

Is it hot today?
Kyō wa atsui desu ka?

It's hot today, don't you think?
Kyō wa atsui desu ne.

The basic sentence remains the same. Only the end markers—*ka* and *ne*—and voice intonation change. Intonation is critical in Japanese. The only way to learn it properly is by listening to spoken Japanese and observing context. Listen to the conversation all around you.

ASKING A QUESTION

Asking questions in a strange language can be intimidating, given that success is anything but guaranteed. And for most Japanese people, being approached by foreigners can be equally intimidating. Their first worry is that they'll be addressed in English, and expected to reply in kind. The second worry is that there'll be communication problems, failure, and loss of face.

If asking a question, always precede it by acknowledging your rudeness with *Shitsurei desu ga.* Alternatively, *Sumimasen* ga can be used. *Shitsurei* and *sumimasen* can be used to apologize for just about anything, from addressing a stranger on the street, to spilling a drink on your date's lap. *Shitsurei shimasu* apologizes for something the speaker is doing while he speaks; *shitsurei shimashita* apologizes for something already done.

If making a request, be aware that properly asking a favor or making a request requires a certain amount of diplomacy. In Japanese, one ideally need not explicitly state a request. An understood and shared context, and a hesitant intonation, make the request obvious. It's good to sound apologetic and unsure, as this can convey politeness at least as effectively as correct grammar and verb conjugation.

To summarize, before springing a question in Japanese upon the unsuspecting, preface it with a smile and apologies, spoken graciously and unaggressively:

Sumimasen. (Excuse me . . .)
   or
Shitsurei desu ga. (I'm being rude, but. . .)

And when all is finished, successful or not, bow your head slightly and say *Dōmo arigato gozaimashita*, which means "Thank you very much."

The directness of the question "Why?" poses problems for many Japanese. It's a confrontational query. One shouldn't have to ask why about most things; the answer either is irrelevant, or obvious from clues with which the speaker has littered the conversation.

what	nan/nani	何	**how far**	dono kurai	どのくらい
when	itsu	いつ	**how long**	dono kurai	どのくらい
where	doko	どこ	**how many**	ikutsu	いくつ
which	dochira	どちら	**how much**	ikura	いくら
who	dare	誰	**what time**	nanji ni	何時に
why	naze	なぜ			

Naturally, when traveling, you'll want and need to ask where places and things are. In Japanese, in which politeness is all-important, asking where has a normal form, doko, and a polite form (dochira, which can also mean who).

(Toire wa) Doko desu ka? (normal)

(Toire wa) Dochira desu ka? (polite)

As a guest or a special stranger, a foreigner will most likely be questioned with *dochira*, adding to the novice Japanese speaker's confusion: are they being asked who, or where?

Word order in questions generally, though not always, goes like this: **Subject** (if there is one), **interrogative keyword** (who, what, where, why, when), then **verb**. For instance:

Where is the toilet?	Who is it?
(Toire wa) Doko desu ka?	*Dare desu ka?*

THE WRITTEN WORD

As mentioned earlier, written Japanese is where the real language barrier springs up for many people. This hellishly complicated system combines four discrete elements:

KANJI: The core of Japan's writing system. Kanji came from China in the 4th century A.D., and have been modified greatly over the ensuing centuries. Most kanji have at least two pronunciations each: one or more original Chinese pronunciations, and one or more home-grown, Japanese pronunciations.

HIRAGANA: A phonetic writing system used for words or word parts for which there are no kanji. Also often used in place of difficult kanji that even Japanese adults may not be able to read, or in lieu of simple kanji that children and foreigners might not be able to read.

KATAKANA: A phonetic writing system used for words of foreign origin, or for emphasizing Japanese ones. Katakana may be thought of as playing a role akin to that of italics in English.

ROMAJI: Roman letters, used mainly to add an aura of worldliness or trendiness to Japanese words. On a related note, English with utterly bizarre usage surfaces everywhere, from T-shirts to storefronts.

JAPANESE SYLLABARIES

R: Romaji   **H**: Hiragana   **K**: Katakana

R	H	K	R	H	K	R	H	K	R	H	K	R	H	K
a	あ	ア	i	い	イ	u	う	ウ	e	え	エ	o	お	オ
ka	か	カ	ki	き	キ	ku	く	ク	ke	け	ケ	ko	こ	コ
sa	さ	サ	shi	し	シ	su	す	ス	se	せ	セ	so	そ	ソ
ta	た	タ	chi	ち	チ	tsu	つ	ツ	te	て	テ	to	と	ト
na	な	ナ	ni	に	ニ	nu	ぬ	ヌ	ne	ね	ネ	no	の	ノ
ha	は	ハ	hi	ひ	ヒ	fu	ふ	フ	he	へ	ヘ	ho	ほ	ホ
ma	ま	マ	mi	み	ミ	mu	む	ム	me	め	メ	mo	も	モ
ya	や	ヤ				yu	ゆ	ユ				yo	よ	ヨ
ra	ら	ラ	ri	り	リ	ru	る	ル	re	れ	レ	ro	ろ	ロ
wa	わ	ワ										(w)o	を	ヲ
n	ん	ン												
ga	が	ガ	gi	ぎ	ギ	gu	ぐ	グ	ge	げ	ゲ	go	ご	ゴ
za	ざ	ザ	ji	じ	ジ	zu	ず	ズ	ze	ぜ	ゼ	zo	ぞ	ゾ
da	だ	ダ	ji	ぢ	ヂ	zu	づ	ヅ	de	で	デ	do	ど	ド
ba	ば	バ	bi	び	ビ	bu	ぶ	ブ	be	べ	ベ	bo	ぼ	ボ
pa	ぱ	パ	pi	ぴ	ピ	pu	ぷ	プ	pe	ぺ	ペ	po	ぽ	ポ

R	H	K	R	H	K	R	H	K
kya	きゃ	キャ	kyu	きゅ	キュ	kyo	きょ	キョ
sha	しゃ	シャ	shu	しゅ	シュ	sho	しょ	ショ
cha	ちゃ	チャ	chu	ちゅ	チュ	cho	ちょ	チョ
nya	にゃ	ニャ	nyu	にゅ	ニュ	nyo	にょ	ニョ
hya	ひゃ	ヒャ	hyu	ひゅ	ヒャ	hyo	ひょ	ヒョ
mya	みゃ	ミャ	myu	みゅ	ミュ	myo	みょ	ミョ
rya	りゃ	リャ	ryu	りゅ	リュ	ryo	りょ	リョ
gya	ぎゃ	ギャ	gyu	ぎゅ	ギュ	gyo	ぎょ	ギョ
ja	じゃ	ジャ	ju	じゅ	ジュ	jo	じょ	ジョ
bya	びゃ	ビョ	byu	びゅ	ビュ	byo	びょ	ビョ
pya	ぴゃ	ピャ	pyu	ぴゅ	ピュ	pyo	ぴょ	ピョ

NUMBERS

And now the numbers.

The wimpy or lazy may just prefer moving onward, forgetting this whole lot. Japanese numbers are not especially simple. But navigating through Japan, as in any country, requires some familiarity with numbers.

There are two different ways to express numbers in Japanese. First, as in Western languages, there are Arabic numerals: 1, 2, 3, and so on. Numbers can also be written as Chinese characters, which might be thought of as representing numbers as words, like writing out the word "three," rather than 3.

sūji
numerals

Numbers in Japanese are divided slightly differently than English numbers. Like English, Japanese has units of tens, hundreds, and thousands. From there, however, it goes on to use ten-thousands, hundred-millions, and trillions. The number 20,000 is not expressed as *ni ju sen*, or twenty thousand, but as *ni man*, or two ten-thousands. The Japanese expression for 1,000,000 is *hyaku man*, or one hundred ten-thousands, rather than a million.

The number four has two pronunciations, *shi* and *yon*, but as shi is a homonym for "death," *yon* is more commonly used. Seven also has two pronunciations, *nana* and *shichi*, with *nana* usually taking precedence.

Confusing? It gets even more so.

BASIC NUMBERS

0	rei	零	50	go jū	五十
0	zero	ゼロ	60	roku jū	六十
1	ichi	一	70	nana jū	七十
2	ni	二	80	hachi jū	八十
3	san	三	90	kyū jū	九十
4	yon, shi	四	100	hyaku	百
5	go	五	200	ni hyaku	二百
6	roku	六	300	san byaku	三百
7	nana. shichi	七	400	yon hyaku	四百
8	hachi	八	500	go hyaku	五百
9	ku, kyū	九	600	roppyaku	六百
10	jū	十	700	nana hyaku	七百
11	jū ichi	十一	800	happyaku	八百
14	jū yon	十四	900	kyū hyaku	九百
20	ni jū	二十	1,000	sen	千
21	ni jū ichi	二十一	2,000	ni sen	二千
22	ni jū ni	二十二	3,000	san zen	三千
23	ni jū san	二十三	4,000	yon sen	四千
24	ni jū yon	二十四	5,000	go sen	五千
25	ni jū go	二十五	6,000	roku sen	六千
26	ni jū roku	二十六	7,000	nana sen	七千
27	ni jū shichi	二十七	8,000	hassen	八千
28	ni jū hachi	二十八	9,000	kyū sen	九千
29	ni jū kyū	二十九	10,000	man	万
30	san jū	三十	100,000	jū man	十万
40	yon jū	四十	1,000,000	hyaku man	百万

LENGTH	WEIGHT	AREA, WIDTH	SPEED
長さ	重さ	広さ	速さ
nagasa	omosa	hirosa	hayasa
HEIGHT	**WEIGHT**	**VOLUME**	**DEPTH**
高さ	(people only)	体積	深さ
takasa	体重	taiseki	fukasa
	taijū		

COUNTING THINGS

Counting things in Japanese is more complicated than doing so in English. Rather than just saying a number and then an object, in Japanese you must also add a suffix called a "counter." To say "two books," (book is "*hon*" in Japanese), you wouldn't just say *ni hon*. You would add the suffix -*satsu*—the counter for books—and say *hon ni-satsu*.

There are many different counters for different types of objects. Some counters are applied to objects of certain shapes. –*mai* is a counter that can be used for any flat object, be it a miror or a pizza. *Kagami go-mai* means "five mirrors," while *pizza ichi-mai* means "one pizza." Other counters are object-specific. Objects that have their own counters include guns (-*chō*) and even chopsticks (-*zen*).

Being able to use appropriate counters is a matter of sheer memory power. Fortunately, there is a simpler (somewhat, anyway) system for counting fewer than ten objects other than people.

1	hitotsu	一つ	6	muttsu	六つ
2	futatsu	二つ	7	nanatsu	七つ
3	mittsu	三つ	8	yattsu	八つ
4	yottsu	四つ	9	kokonotsu	九つ
5	itsutsu	五つ	10	tō	十

FLAT THINGS		
-MAI -枚		
paper, cloth, pizza, window glass		
1	ichi-mai	一枚
2	ni-mai	二枚
3	san-mai	三枚
4	yon-mai	四枚
5	go-mai	五枚
6	roku-mai	六枚
7	nana-mai	七枚
8	hachi-mai	八枚
9	kyū-mai	九枚
10	jū-mai	十枚

CONTAINERS		
-HAI, -PAI -杯		
cups, bowls, glasses		
1	ippai	一杯
2	ni-hai	二杯
3	san-bai	三杯
4	yon-hai	四杯
5	go-hai	五杯
6	roppai	六杯
7	nana-hai	七杯
8	hachi-hai	八杯
9	kyū-hai	九杯
10	jippai	十杯

LONG & THIN ITEMS		
-HON, -PON -本 pencils, pens, bottles		
1	ippon	一本
2	nihon	二本
3	san-bon	三本
4	yon-hon	四本
5	go-hon	五本
6	roppon	六本
7	nana-hon	七本
8	hachi-hon	八本
9	kyū-hon	九本
10	jippon	十本

PEOPLE		
-NIN -人 people		
1	hitori	一人
2	futari	二人
3	san-nin	三人
4	yo-nin	四人
5	go-nin	五人
6	roku-nin	六人
7	nana-nin	七人
8	hachi-nin	八人
9	kyū-nin	九人
10	jū-nin	十人

PUBLICATIONS		
-SATSU -冊 magazines, books		
1	issatsu	一冊
2	ni-satsu	二冊
3	san-satsu	三冊
4	yon-satsu	四冊
5	go-satsu	五冊
6	roku-satsu	六冊
7	nana-satsu	七冊
8	hassatsu	八冊
9	kyū-satsu	九冊
10	jissatsu	十冊

SPHERES & CUBES		
-KO -個 oranges, baseballs, boxes		
1	ikko	一個
2	ni-ko	二個
3	san-ko	三個
4	yon-ko	四個
5	go-ko	五個
6	rokko	六個
7	nana-ko	七個
8	hakko	八個
9	kyū-ko	九個
10	jikko	十個

ESSENTIAL VERBS

to count 数える kazoeru	to calculate 計算する keisan suru	to add up 合計する gōkei suru

THE CLOCK

When is it/that?	(Sore wa) Itsu desu ka?	(それは) いつですか。
When was it/that?	(Sore wa) Itsu deshita ka?	(それは) いつでしたか。
What time is it?	Ima nan ji desu ka?	今何時ですか。
It's ~.	~ desu	〜です。
1 o'clock	ichi ji	一時
2 o'clock	ni ji	二時
3 o'clock	san ji	三時
4 o'clock	yo ji	四時
5 o'clock	go ji	五時
6 o'clock	roku ji	六時
7 o'clock	shichi ji	七時
8 o'clock	hachi ji	八時
9 o'clock	ku ji	九時
10 o'clock	jū ji	十時
11 o'clock	jū ichi ji	十一時
12 o'clock	jū ni ji	十二時

at 1 o'clock	ichi ji ni	一時に
at about 1 o'clock	ichi ji goro ni	一時ごろに
at 1 o'clock sharp	ichiji chōdo ni	一時ちょうどに
~ a.m.	gozen ~	午前〜
~ p.m.	gogo ~	午後〜
half past ~	~ han	〜半
before ~	~ mae	〜前
after ~	~ sugi	〜過ぎ
until ~	~ made	〜まで
by ~	~ made ni	〜までに

What time is it from?	Nan ji kara desu ka?	何時からですか。
It's from ~.	~ kara desu.	〜からです。
What time is it until?	Nan ji made desu ka?	何時までですか。
It's until ~.	~ made desu.	〜までです。

AMOUNT OF TIME

How long will/does it take?	Dono kurai kakarimasu ka?	どのくらいかかりますか。
It takes/will take ~.	~ kakarimasu.	〜かかります。
How long did it take?	Dono kurai kakarimashita ka?	どのくらいかかりましたか。
It took ~.	~ kakarimashita.	〜かかりました。
When will it be ready?	Itsu dekimasu ka?	いつできますか。

MINUTE	funkan	分間	HOUR	jikan	時間
1 minute	ippunkan	一分間	1 hour	ichi jikan	一時間
2 minutes	ni funkan	二分間	2 hours	ni jikan	二時間
3 minutes	san punkan	三分間	6 hours	roku jikan	六時間
4 minutes	yon punkan	四分間	12 hours	jū ni jikan	十二時間
5 minutes	go funkan	五分間	every ~	~ goto	〜ごと
6 minutes	roppunkan	六分間	exactly ~	~ chōdo	〜ちょうど
7 minutes	nana funkan	七分間	about ~	~ yaku	〜約
8 minutes	happunkan	八分間	within ~	~ inai	〜以内
9 minutes	kyūfunkan	九分間	over ~	~ ijō	〜以上
10 minutes	jippunkan	十分間	~ ago	~ mae	〜前
30 minutes	san jippunkan	三十分間	~ later	~ go	〜後
several minutes	sūfunkan	数分間	several hours	sūjikan	数時間

DAY	nichikan/-kakan	日間	WEEK	shūkan	週間
1 day	ichi nichi	一日	1 week	isshūkan	一週間
2 days	futsukakan	二日間	2 weeks	ni shūkan	二週間
3 days	mikkakan	三日間	3 weeks	san shūkan	三週間
several days	sūjitsukan	数日間	several weeks	sūshūkan	数週間

MONTH	-ka getsukan	ヵ月間	YEAR	nenkan	年間
1 month	ikka getsukan	一ヵ月間	half a year	hantoshikan	半年間
2 months	ni-ka getsukan	二ヵ月間	1 year	ichi nenkan	一年間
3 months	san-ka getsukan	三ヵ月間	2 years	ni nenkan	二年間
several months	sū-ka getsukan	数ヵ月間	several years	sū nenkan	数年間

CALENDAR

When is it/that?	(Sore wa) Itsu desu ka?	(それは) いつですか。
When was it/that?	(Sore wa) Itsu deshita ka?	(それは) いつでしたか。
What day is it?	Nan yōbi desu ka?	何曜日ですか。
It's ~.	~ desu.	〜です。
Monday	Getsuyōbi	月曜日
Tuesday	Kayōbi	火曜日
Wednesday	Suiyōbi	水曜日
Thursday	Mokuyōbi	木曜日
Friday	Kinyōbi	金曜日
Saturday	Doyōbi	土曜日
Sunday	Nichiyōbi	日曜日

What month is it?	Nan gatsu desu ka?	何月ですか。
It's ~.	~ desu.	〜です。
January	Ichigatsu	一月
February	Nigatsu	二月
March	Sangatsu	三月
April	Shigatsu	四月
May	Gogatsu	五月
June	Rokugatsu	六月
July	Shichigatsu	七月
August	Hachigatsu	八月
September	Kugatsu	九月
October	Jūgatsu	十月
November	Jūichigatsu	十一月
December	Jūnigatsu	十二月

daytime	hiruma	昼間
weekday	heijitsu	平日
every day	mainichi	毎日
every other day	ichi nichi oki	一日おき
half a day	hannichi	半日

morning	asa	朝
A.M.	gozen	午前
noon	hiru	昼
afternoon, P.M.	gogo	午後
evening, late afternoon	yūgata	夕方
evening, night	yoru	夜
middle of the night	mayonaka	真夜中
midnight	yonaka	夜中
last Monday	senshū no Getsuyōbi	先週の月曜日
this Monday	konshū no Getsuyōbi	今週の月曜日
next Monday	raishū no Getsuyōbi	来週の月曜日
day before yesterday	ototoi	一昨日
yesterday	kinō	昨日
today	kyō	今日
this morning	kesa	今朝
tonight/this evening	kon'ya	今夜
tonight/this evening	konban	今晩
tomorrow	ashita	明日
tomorrow morning	ashita no asa	明日の朝
day after tomorrow	asatte	明後日

WEEK	shū	週
every week	maishū	毎週
week before last	sensenshū	先々週
last week	senshū	先週
this week	konshū	今週
next week	raishū	来週
week after next	saraishū	再来週
every other week	isshūkan oki	一週間おき
weekday	heijitsu	平日
weekend	shūmatsu	週末

BASICS

MONTH	tsuki, gatsu, getsu	月
every month	maitsuki	毎月
every other month	ikkagetsu oki	一ヵ月おき
first third of a month	jōjun	上旬
middle third of a month	chūjun	中旬
last third of a month	gejun	下旬
end of the month	getsumatsu	月末
two months ago	sensengetsu	先々月
last month	sengetsu	先月
this month	kongetsu	今月
next month	raigetsu	来月
month after next	saraigetsu	再来月
middle of next month	raigetsu no naka goro	来月の中ごろ
end of this month	kongetsu no sue	今月の末

YEAR	toshi	年
what year	nan nen	何年
every year	maitoshi	毎年
every other year	ichinen oki	一年おき
half a year	hantoshi	半年
year before last	ototoshi, issaku nen	おととし, 一昨年
last year	kyonen	去年
this year	kotoshi	今年
next year	rainen	来年
year after next	sarainen	再来年
leap year	urū doshi	閏年
end of the year	nenmatsu	年末

present times	gendai	現代
present, now	genzai	現在
these days, recently	saikin	最近
future	mirai	未来
future, days yet to come	shōrai	将来

Basics
TALKING

A first meeting between Japanese and Western business people can resemble a bad comedy. The Japanese want to shake hands and practice their English, the foreigners want to bow and try their memorized Japanese greetings. Each party wants to please the other; neither party wants to look stupid.

However the initial pleasantries may end up, the foreigners typically want to get down to business right away, while the Japanese want to continue the pleasantries. In Japan, a considerable amount of time is devoted—nearly religiously—toward small talk and the establishment of trust and confidence. A Japanese businessman may spend years developing a relationship with a potential client or partner before settling down to business.

Especially for the Westerner in a hurry, nurturing friendships with Japanese can be a puzzling experience. The rules are different. One can know a Japanese person for years, considering him a good friend, and yet never see the front door of his home.

Japanese may wear Western clothes, spend years studying English, and eat American fast-food, but they are not Westerners. Don't evaluate personal relationships with Japanese according to Western precepts; there are thinking processes and worldviews that are simply too different. Just as there are aspects of being Japanese that elude our understanding, Japanese can sometimes be bewildered by Western behavior.

kaiwa
conversation

POLITENESS AND THE GROUP

Fundamental to the Japanese way of life is *The Group* and one's place within—or outside—it. Where you stand in relation to *The Group*—family, company, or otherwise—determines the politeness of your speech. This overriding concern with knowing proper place helps explain Japanese people's near-fanaticism about exchanging business cards, or *meishi*. A *meishi* tells a Japanese all he needs to know about his counterpart's status relative to his own and enables him to select the appropriate mode of speech and etiquette. Interpersonal communication in Japan is a constant game of comparing statuses, so that everybody can play his or her proper social role.

The existence of levels of politeness, from gruff to extremely polite language, makes it dangerously easy for non-Japanese to sound rude or presumptuous by slipping up and using inappropriate diction. For example, just for expressing the first-person pronoun "I," young men can choose among four different words, each conveying different levels of politeness and self-assertion. (From polite to not: *watakushi*, *watashi*, *boku*, *ore*.) Sex and age of a speaker notwithstanding, the formality of a sentence is determined chiefly by its verb(s). Verbs conjugated with a *-masu* ending, of which this book makes extensive use, are always polite and acceptable. Be aware, though, that *-masu* is but the tip of the politeness iceberg; honorific conjugations and constructions abound, causing confusion not only for non-Japanese, but even for native speakers of the language. Fortunately, this is a fine point with which most visitors need not concern themselves. Usually.

If a Japanese person chooses to bring you into his or her group—whether for a couple of drinks after a chance encounter on the train or into a long-term business relationship—his commitment to the relationship is solid. Make no mistake: Japanese feel very keenly the responsibilities of friendship and relationships with people whom they view as reliable friends or business partners. (Hence the time taken in nurturing relationships.) To reciprocate with a frivolous or flippant attitude regarding a relationship is an insult.

BASIC EXPRESSIONS

Japanese has some basic words and expressions that help smooth one's way in life. Some expressions only hint or suggest at one's intended meaning, leaving much unsaid. Others are short and succinct. Listen to the hubbub around you; these expressions pop up continually and consistently. Note that there are both formal and informal forms; both will be heard in conversation.

I understand.	I don't understand.
Wakarimashita.	*Wakarimasen.*
Wakatta. (informal)	*Wakaranai.* (informal)
That's correct.	That's incorrect.
Sō desu.	*Sō de wa arimasen.*
Sō. (informal)	*Sō ja nai.* (informal)
It's okay.	It's not okay.
Ii desu.	*Dame desu.*
Ii. (informal)	*Dame da.* (informal)
I like it.	I don't like it.
Suki desu.	*Suki de wa arimasen.*
Suki da. (informal)	*Suki ja nai.* (informal)
Is there a/an . . . ?	Is (Name) there/here?
. . . wa arimasu ka?	*(Name)-san wa imasu ka?*

chotto

A word of diverse use and pragmatic vagueness. *Chotto* literally means "a little," but can be used to express a wide variety of meanings, including a small amount of time, a small amount of something, and even regrets. If you want to turn down a request or offer, just saying *chotto* and letting it trail off is often enough to make clear that you want or need to decline. (An explanation, however, should soon follow.) In this sense, *chotto* can be thought of as similar to the English phrase, "I'm afraid . . ."

Please wait a bit.	I'm afraid that's impossible.
Chotto matte kudasai.	*Chotto muri desu ne.*

hai

A source of great misunderstanding by foreigners, who often think it means an unqualified yes. It can mean this, but it is also used frequently to acknowledge what someone else has said. In this case, it doesn't mean agreement, just that the words have been heard.

Yes, I understand.	Yes.
Hai, wakarimashita.	*Hai.*

iie

Usually a definitive no, or used to disagree with what has just been said. Not to be confused with *ē*, which is a casual yes.

No, not yet.	No, I don't have it.
Iie, mada desu.	*Iie, motte imasen.*

dōmo

Has a number of meanings, but in most situations that a traveler hears it, *dōmo* is a casual thanks, or a greeting.

Thanks.	Hi!
Dōmo (arigatō).	*Aa! Dōmo.*

ii

Literally means "good," but like several of the other words described above, is much more versatile than that. It can be used to indicate that something is acceptable or even excellent. On the other hand, it can be used to reject or refuse something (implying that the status quo is okay).

It's fine weather, isn't it?	Would you like a beer?
Ii tenki desu ne.	*Biiru wa ikaga desu ka?*

Yes, it's okay.	No, thanks, I'm fine.
Hai, ii desu.	*Iie, ii desu.*

Sō desu ka?

This phrase, which means, "Oh, really," is one of the conversation "fillers" known in Japanese as *aizuchi*, grunts and phrases that one uses to confirm that he is listening to a speaker. (*Hai* and *Wakarimashita* also often fall into the category of *aizuchi*.) Variations on it include "Ā, sō desu ka," and the more informal "So ka?"

Sō desu ne.

Another conversational standard in the same league as *Sō desu ka?* If this phrase is said with a rising intonation, the speaker is seeking agreement from the listener. If the pitch drops, then the speaker is probably in agreement with whatever's been said by the other person.

sore

Usually translated simply as "That." It can refer either to an idea or an object.

That's right.	I'm against that.
Sore wa sō desu.	*Sore ni wa hantai desu.*
That's good, isn't it.	That's my wallet.
Sore wa ii desu ne.	*Sore wa watashi no saifu desu.*
That's no good.	That's true, but I'm afraid . . .
Sore wa dame desu.	*Sore wa sō desu ga...*

kekkō

A word that can be either positive or negative, depending upon context. It can express satisfaction with something, or it can politely decline an offer.

Yes, I'm happy with it.	No, that's okay, thanks.
Hai, kekkō desu.	*Iie, kekkō desu.*

GREETINGS

As anywhere, greetings in Japan can be either vacuous formalities or sincere inquiries. *Ohayō gozaimasu*, literally meaning "It is early," is an appropriate morning greeting. *Konnichi wa*, which may be thought of as simply "hello," is especially appropriate in the afternoon, but can be used at any time, day or night. In the evening, *konban wa* is used upon greeting, while *o-yasumi nasai* serves as a parting phrase.

When you greet someone, a slight dip of your head can add to your greeting's politeness. Note that among family and friends, however, these standard greetings are too stiff and formal.

Good morning.	Ohayō gozaimasu.	おはようございます。
Good afternoon.	Konnichi wa.	こんにちは。
Good evening.	Konban wa.	こんばんは。

GOOD-BYE

On the telephone, goodbyes among acquaintances and associates are rather brusque by Western standards, especially in the office. It's said that this habit developed in the 1950s and 1960s, when Japanese businessmen traveling overseas cut costs by eliminating telephone chitchat on phone calls to their home offices in Tokyo.

The well known expression *sayōnara* carries a certain amount of finality and sometimes regret to it, and so it is not said among family and friends in everyday situations. Common especially among young women and children is a simple *bai-bai*, similar to English. Another casual and friendly goodbye is *Ja, mata*, meaning "see you later."

Good night. *(upon departing)*	O-yasumi nasai.	おやすみなさい。
Good-bye. *(leaving early)*	Sumimasen ga o-saki ni shitsurei shimasu.	すみませんがお先に失礼します。
I've got to go now.	Sore de wa soro-soro shitsurei shimasu.	それではそろそろ失礼します。
I've got to get up early, so I must go.	Ashita no asa hayai no de, kono hen de shitsurei shimasu.	明日の朝早いのでこの辺で失礼します。

ENCOUNTERS

For the first introduction, the routine is pretty standard:

My name is ~.	~ desu.	〜です。
This is ~.	Kochira wa ~-san desu.	こちらは〜さんです。
Nice to meet you. *(1st person)*	Hajimemashite, dōzo yoroshiku.	はじめまして、どうぞよろしく。
Nice to meet you too. *(2nd person)*	Kochira koso dōzo yoroshiku.	こちらこそどうぞよろしく。

This way, please.	Kochira e dōzo.	こちらへどうぞ。
After you, please.	O-saki ni dōzo.	お先にどうぞ。
Please sit down.	Dōzo o-suwari kudasai.	どうぞお座り下さい。
Just a moment.	Chotto matte kudasai.	ちょっと待って下さい。
Please come in.	Dōzo o-hairi kudasai.	どうぞお入り下さい。
when entering a store/ house and summoning someone	Gomen kudasai.	ごめん下さい。

Excuse me, are you Mr. /Ms. ~?	Shitsurei desu ga, ~-san desu ka?	失礼ですが、〜さんですか。
Are you a/an *(nationality)*?	~jin desu ka?	〜人ですか。
I'm a/an *(nationality)*.	~jin desu.	〜人です。
I'm from ~.	~ kara kimashita.	〜から来ました。
Australia	Ōsutoraria	オーストラリア
Canada	Kanada	カナダ
England	Igirisu	イギリス
France	Furansu	フランス
Germany	Doitsu	ドイツ
Italy	Itaria	イタリア
Malaysia	Marēshia	マレーシア
New Zealand	Nyū Jiirando	ニュージーランド
Singapore	Shingapōru	シンガポール
United States	Amerika	アメリカ

Questions about your life and interests may be no more than idle chatter, but realize also that for Japanese, small talk is part of gaining trust and establishing relationships. However, be aware that, depending on the situation, some personal questions may not appropriate. In particular, avoid asking overly personal questions of business or casual acquaintances.

May I have your name?	O-namae wa nan to osshaimasu ka?	お名前は何とおっしゃいますか。
My name is ~.	~ desu.	～です。
This is my (business) card.	Meishi desu.	名刺です。
Where are you from?	O-kuni wa dochira desu ka?	お国はどちらですか。
Where do you live?	O-sumai wa dochira desu ka?	お住まいはどちらですか。
Are you alone?	Hitori desu ka?	一人ですか。
Are you married?	Kekkon shite imasu ka?	結婚していますか。
Are you single?	Dokushin desu ka?	独身ですか。
Where were you born?	O-umare wa dochira desu ka?	お生まれはどちらですか。
When were you born?	Nan nen umare desu ka?	何年生まれですか。
When is your birthday?	O-tanjōbi wa itsu desu ka?	お誕生日はいつですか。
Where are you staying?	Dochira e o-tomari desu ka?	どちらへお泊まりですか。
When did you come to Japan?	Itsu Nihon ni kimashita ka?	いつ日本に来ましたか。
How long have you been here?	Dono kurai ni narimasu ka?	どのくらいになりますか。
How long will you stay?	Dono kurai irassharu yotei desu ka?	どのくらいいらっしゃる予定ですか。
I plan to stay ~ days.	~ nichikan taizai suru yotei desu.	～日間滞在する予定です。
Is this your first time (in Japan)?	(Nihon wa) Hajimete desu ka?	(日本は)初めてですか。
This is my first visit.	Hajimete desu.	初めてです。
This is my second visit.	Nikaime desu.	二回目です。
Do you like Japan?	Nihon ga suki desu ka?	日本が好きですか。
Why did you come to Japan?	Naze Nihon e irashita n'desu ka?	なぜ、日本へいらしたんですか。
on business	shigoto de	仕事で
on vacation	kyūka de	休暇で
to study Japanese	Nihongo o benkyō suru tame ni	日本語を勉強するために
to study Japanese culture	Nihon no bunka o benkyō suru tame ni	日本の文化を勉強するために
When are you leaving?	Go-shuppatsu wa itsu desu ka?	ご出発はいつですか。
When are you returning to your country?	Go-kikoku wa itsu desu ka?	ご帰国はいつですか。

APOLOGIES

The Japanese are unsurpassed in expressing social apologies. Done correctly, it is a fine art of nuance. Older women, especially, seem to take pleasure in trying to outdo one another with the most convincing apology and politeness, sometimes forgetting the reason (usually trivial) for having started it all in the first place.

Excuse me. *(when prefacing question, request)*	Sumimasen ga.	すみませんが。
Excuse me. *(when rude or committing a faux pas)*	Shitsurei shimashita.	失礼しました。
Excuse me, but I have a question.	Sumimasen ga shitsumon ga aru n'desu ga.	すみませんが質問があるんですが。
I beg your pardon. *(not understanding what's been said)*	Sumimasen ga mō ichido itte kudasai.	すみませんがもう一度言って下さい。

I'm sorry/Excuse me.	Shitsurei desu ga.	失礼ですが。
I'm sorry/Excuse me.	Sumimasen.	すみません。
I'm sorry that I broke it.	Kowashite shimatte gomen nasai.	こわしてしまってごめんなさい。
Sorry I can't meet you.	O-ai dekinakute zannen desu.	お会いできなくて残念です。
Sorry that I can't visit you.	Ukagaenakute sumimasen.	うかがえなくてすみません。
Sorry to be late.	Osoku natte gomen nasai.	遅くなってごめんなさい。
Sorry I'm going to be late.	Chotto okureru n'desu ga.	ちょっと遅れるんですが。
Sorry I don't have time.	Chotto jikan ga nai n'desu ga.	ちょっと時間がないんですが。
Sorry I'm too busy.	Chotto isogashii n'desu ga.	ちょっと忙しいんですが。
Sorry for disturbing you when you're so busy.	O-isogashii tokoro ni sumimasen.	お忙しいところにすみません。
Sorry I can't help you.	Chotto o-yaku ni tatenai n'desu ga.	ちょっとお役に立てないんですが。
Sorry I couldn't help you.	O-yaku ni tatenakute sumimasen.	お役に立てなくてすみません。
Sorry I couldn't write to you earlier.	O-henji ga okurete sumimasen.	お返事が遅れてすみません。
Sorry to hear about that.	Sore wa zannen desu.	それは残念です。
I'm really very sorry.	Hontō ni mōshi wake arimasen.	本当に申し訳ありません。
It was my fault. *(2nd person)*	Watashi no hō koso sumimasen.	私の方こそすみません。

SAYING NO

Saying "no" explicitly is difficult for most Japanese, as directness counters the ideals of maintaining harmony and face. Instead, the Japanese language is studded with well-understood (by Japanese) cues for indirectly communicating the idea of no. For example, in refusing an invitation to do something later in the day, either socially or professionally, one might simply reply "*Kyō wa chotto*," or "I'm afraid, . . ." and that's it. Message understood. Next subject.

Sorry, but . . . *(No, I can't)*	Ano chotto.	あのちょっと。
Sorry, but I'm busy on ~.	Sumimasen. ~ wa chotto.	すみません。〜はちょっと。
Sorry, but I already have something to do.	Ano chotto yōji ga arimashite.	あのちょっと用事がありまして。
Sorry, but I won't be able to come.	Zannen desu ga.	残念ですが。
I can't do it today.	Kyō wa chotto.	今日はちょっと。
Let's do it some other time.	Tsugi no kikai ni zehi onegai.	次の機会にぜひお願いします。
I've got previous plans.	Sen'yaku ga arimasu no de.	先約がありますので。
Sorry, I don't know.	Chotto wakaranai n'desu ga.	ちょっとわからないんですが。
Sorry, I don't have time.	Chotto jikan ga nai n'desu ga.	ちょっと時間がないんですが。
Sorry, I'm too busy.	Chotto isogashii n'desu ga.	ちょっと忙しいんですが。
Sorry, I can't help you.	Chotto o-yaku ni tatenai n'desu ga.	ちょっとお役に立てないんですが。
Sorry, s/he isn't here now.	Chotto ima inai n'desu ga.	ちょっと今いないんですが。

No, thanks. *(rejecting food)*	Mō kekkō desu.	もうけっこうです。
Not for me, thanks.	Watashi wa kekkō desu.	私はけっこうです。
Thanks, but I don't like/ need/want ~.	~ wa kekkō desu.	〜はけっこうです。
No, thanks, I don't smoke.	Tabako wa kekkō desu.	たばこはけっこうです。
No, thanks, I don't drink.	O-sake wa kekkō desu	お酒はけっこうです。

THANK YOU

As with apologies, expressing a proper thank-you requires a talent for conveying delicate shades of meaning. For most of us, however, the polite Dōmo *arigatō gozaimashita* is adequate. More casual yet still polite is the shorter *Arigatō gozaimashita*. Very casual yet frequently used among strangers is *arigatō* or even *dōmo*. Again, as with other pleasantries, a slight bow or dip of the head adds to the politeness.

If you're meeting someone whom you've met before, but this time in a formal situation, it's important to make a reference to the previous encounter, and to offer thanks for the help and kindness you received then, even if there wasn't any. A ritual, for sure, but it conveys your recognition of the relationship and appreciation for its continuity.

Thank you very much.	Arigatō gozaimashita.	ありがとうございました。
Thank you for your kindness.	Iro-iro arigatō gozaimashita.	いろいろありがとうございました。
Thank you for your letter.	O-tegami arigatō gozaimashita.	お手紙ありがとうございました。
Thank you for your reply.	O-henji arigatō gozaimashita.	お返事ありがとうございました。
Thank you for all your help.	Iro-iro o-sewa ni narimashita.	いろいろお世話になりました。
Thank you for calling me.	O-denwa arigatō gozaimashita.	お電話ありがとうございました。
Thank you for helping me.	O-tetsudai itadakimashite arigatō gozaimashita.	お手伝いいただきましてありがとうございました。
Thank you for inviting me.	Go-shōtai arigatō gozaimashita.	ご招待ありがとうございました。
Thank you for the other day.	SenjItsu wa arigatō gozaimashita.	先日はありがとうございました。

AIZUCHI

It's embarrassing when a kind stranger is graciously offering help, and you don't understand a single thing being said, yet you pretend you do. If you've gotten in over your head in soliciting help, it's difficult to know whether to bolt away or continue the act. If you pick the latter course, play along by offering *aizuchi* (nods, grunts, and other feedback) when the speaker pauses. Just know that Japanese feel considerable responsibility when helping someone, which might explain why they sometimes avoid helping strangers at all.

INVITATIONS

If you're invited to a Japanese home, whether for dinner or a Sunday afternoon visit, definitely accept after a polite amount of hesitation and concern for your intrusion. As a guest, you will be treated royally and enjoy an opportunity to learn much from seeing how Japanese live. (Such an invitation can also reflect a certain degree of acceptance within a group.)

If, however, you are never invited to a friend's or business associate's home, don't take it personally. The home may just be too small and too cluttered for its owner to feel comfortable having company. He may also worry that you'll compare his compact, no-nonsense dwelling with your Western home, which may be palatial in comparison. The fact that most urbanites don't especially like their homes—sometimes just a single room with bath—is reflected in the many evening hours spent in drinking places, coffee shops, and restaurants.

When visiting a home, bring a gift. Something edible (classy prepackaged cookies or cakes, for example) is expected; going empty-handed is impolite. Contrary to what one may expect, however, food brought as a gift is usually not served then and there, or even later and there. It could very well be passed off onto someone else later.

O-miyage, or souvenirs, are the most common kind of gift, given to friends and associates when returning home from a trip. Department stores and train stations devote considerable space to the selling of *o-miyage*, especially individually-wrapped cookies and cakes and local delicacies. In fact, just about anything can be packaged as a gift, whatever the occasion. Department stores, for example, offer gift boxes of common laundry soaps at astounding prices, and packages of fruits, sweets, and alcohol come packaged together in special gift sets.

A final note about gift-giving. Gifts are supposed to be tokens of gratitude. Since one's feelings of indebtedness are so much greater than a measly bauble could properly convey, however, it becomes the giver to say something to diminish the value's gift.

It's tedious even to some Japanese, this rite and guilt of gift-giving.

INVITATIONS

Unless a Japanese acquaintance or business associate has a house or apartment of substantial size, you probably won't be invited to his home. But should you receive an invitation for dinner or a visit, it's best to hesitate in a way suggesting that your presence would be an intrusion. If the invitation persists, then by all means accept.

Would you like to visit my home? 家へいらっしゃいませんか。	**Would you like to have dinner?** 夕食をいっしょにいかがですか。

Isn't it a lot of trouble?	Go-meiwaku de wa arimasen ka?	ごめわくではありませんか。
Won't I be disturbing you?	O-jama de wa arimasen ka?	おじゃまではありませんか。
Are you sure it's okay if I come?	Yoroshii n'desu ka?	よろしいんですか。

It's polite and proper to bring a (wrapped) gift when visiting. Department stores and the larger train stations devote counters to gift purchases (which are also important when returning home from travels). When presenting the gift, diminish the value of the gift with a soft and hesitant voice. It's all part of the humbling ritual and very important.

This is just a little something.	Tsumaranai mono desu ga.	つまらない物ですが。
This is something small, but I hope you'll enjoy It.	Tsumaranai mono desu ga mina-san de meshiagatte kudasai.	つまらない物ですが皆さんで召し上がって下さい。
I don't know if you'll like it, but here is a small gift.	O-suki ka dō ka wakarimasen ga dōzo.	お好きかどうかわかりませんがどうぞ。

Well, I must be going.	Sore de wa watashi wa soro-soro.	それでは私はそろそろ。
I had a great time today.	Kyō wa hontō ni tanoshikatta desu.	今日は本当に楽しかったです。
Thank you for the delicious meal.	Gochisōsama deshita.	ごちそうさまでした。
Thank you for inviting me today.	Kyō wa o-maneki itadakimashite arigatō gozaimashita.	今日はお招きいただきましてありがとうございました。

41

FAMILY

In Japan, it is not uncommon for three generations of family to live the same house under rather intimate conditions. It is a traditional sponsibility of the eldest son to look after his parents in their final years, a responsibility that causes some women to want to avoid marrying eldest sons. (In her own home, the wife is typically subservient to the mother-law, and even visiting sisters-in-law, often not unlike a maid.)

That's ~, isn't it?	Ano kata ga ~-san desu ne.	あの方が～さんですね。
Did you meet ~?	~ o gozonji desu ka?	～をごぞんじですか。
Is this ~?	Kore wa ~ desu ka?	これは～ですか。
This is ~. (e.g., in photo)	Kore wa ~ desu.	これは～です。
an acquaintance	shiriai	知り合い
my friend	tomodachi, yūjin	友達、友人
a friend of ~'s	~ no yūjin	～の友人
a boyfriend/girlfriend, lover	koibito	恋人
my family	kazoku	家族
my spouse	haigūsha	配偶者
my wife	tsuma	妻
my husband	otto	夫
my daughter	musume	娘
my son	musuko	息子
my mother	haha	母
my father	chichi	父

your family	go-kazoku	ご家族
your/his wife	okusan	奥さん
your/her husband	go-shujin	ご主人
your/her daughter	musume-san	娘さん
your/her son	musuko-san	息子さん
your/her parents	go-ryōshin	ご両親
your/her mother	okasan	お母さん
your/her father	otōsan	お父さん
your/her siblings	go-kyōdai	ご兄弟

MY ~

RELATIVES	OLDER SISTER	OLDER BROTHER	GRANDMOTHER
親戚	姉	兄	祖母
shinseki	ane	ani	sobo
SIBLINGS	**YOUNGER SISTER**	**YOUNGER BROTHER**	**GRANDFATHER**
兄弟, 姉妹	妹	弟	祖父
kyōdai, shimai	imōto	otōto	sofu

YOURS/HIS/HER ~

RELATIVES	OLDER SISTER	OLDER BROTHER	GRANDMOTHER
ご親戚	お姉さん	お兄さん	おばあさん
go-shinseki	onēsan	oniisan	obāsan
BROTHERS/ SISTERS	**YOUNGER SISTER**	**YOUNGER BROTHER**	**GRANDFATHER**
ご兄弟, ご姉妹	妹さん	弟さん	おじいさん
go-kyōdai, go-shimai	imōto-san	otōto-san	ojiisan

PEOPLE

PEOPLE, PERSON	BOY	ADULT	WOMAN
人	男の子	大人	女の人
hito	otoko no ko	otona	onna no hito
BABY	**GIRL**	**MIDDLE-AGED PERSON**	**MAN**
赤ちゃん	女の子	中年	男の人
akachan	onna no ko	chūnen	otoko no hito
CHILD, CHILDREN	**YOUNG PEOPLE**	**ELDERLY PERSON**	
子供	若者	お年寄り	
kodomo	wakamono	o-toshiyori	

Where does ~ live?	How old is ~?
～はどちらにお住まいですか。	～はおいくつですか。

43

RELIGION

Do you have a religion?	Nanika shinkō o o-mochi desu ka?	何か信仰をお持ちですか。
I'm a devout believer.	Nesshin-na shinja desu.	熱心な信者です。
I'm not a strong believer.	Amari nesshin de wa arimasen.	あまり熱心ではありません。
I believe in ~.	~ o shinjite imasu.	～を信じています。
atheism	mushinron	無神論
agnosticism	fukachiron	不可知論
Shinto	Shintō	神道
Buddhism	Bukkyō	仏教
Confucianism	Jukyō	儒教
Islam	Isuramukyō	イスラム教
Judaism	Yudayakyō	ユダヤ教
Christianity	Kirisutokyō	キリスト教
Do you attend a ~?	~ e wa ikimasu ka?	～へは行きますか。
Shinto shrine	jinja	神社
Buddhist temple	o-tera	お寺
mosque	mosuku	モスク
church	Kirisuto kyōkai	キリスト教会
synagogue	Yudaya kyōkai	ユダヤ教会

RELIGION 宗教 shūkyō

BIBLE 聖書 seisho

FAMILY ALTAR 仏壇 butsudan

SHRINE GATE 鳥居 torii

BELIEF, FAITH 信仰 shinkō

FAMILY ALTAR *(Shinto)* 神棚 kami dana

BUDDHIST PRIEST お坊さん obōsan

TO PRAY 祈る inoru

GOD 神 (さま) kami (-sama)

SHINTO PRIEST 神主 kannushi

BUDDHIST STATUE 仏像 butsuzō

TO BELIEVE 信じる shinjiru

KORAN コーラン kōran

BUDDHA 仏 (さま) Hotoke (-sama)

GREAT BUDDHA 大仏 Daibutsu

TO BELIEVE IN *(faith)* 信仰する shinkō suru

NAMES

Japan has a long tradition of using titles, rather than names, to address people. In contemporary offices, this practice is still prevalent, with the boss addressed by his title, such as *kachō* (section chief) or *shachō* (president). Teachers and doctors (and others that one wants to butter up) are called *sensei*.

Long ago in the old imperial court, asking a woman's given name was in fact a marriage proposal (a woman back then was identified with regard to her male patron, whether a father, brother, or simply an aristocrat who had taken her under his wing); if she gave it, she was indicating her willingness to marry. It was only after the beginning of Japan's modern period in 1868 that everyone, regardless of economic or social position, was permitted to have a family name; surnames then became mandatory in 1875. Even before then, however, the government maintained a mandatory family register system, and it is still rigorously maintained today.

Family names commonly have between one and three kanji, or Chinese characters.

Most male first names have two kanji characters. Female first names often have one or two syllables plus the suffix *-ko*, meaning "child," which was formerly reserved for aristocrats. The female name is sometimes in kanji, sometimes a mix of kanji and hiragana, and occasionally all hiragana.

The name and Chinese characters selected by parents for a child are usually chosen with an eye toward aligning their meanings with the future qualities to which the parents aspire for their newborn. After the parents choose the kanji from a government-approved list, the name must be added to the family register, which is maintained by the local municipal office. (A family will often check the register of a prospective son or daughter-in-law to confirm an ethnically clean and honorable background.)

Hayashi	Kimura	Mori	Satō	Tanaka	Yamaguchi
林	木村	森	佐藤	田中	山口
Itō	**Kobayashi**	**Murakami**	**Suzuki**	**Ueda**	**Yamamoto**
伊藤	小林	村上	鈴木	上田	山本
Katō	**Matsumoto**	**Nakamura**	**Takahashi**	**Watanabe**	**Yoshida**
加藤	松本	中村	高橋	渡辺	吉田

WORK

What is your job/work?	O-shigoto wa nan desu ka?	お仕事はなんですか。
Where do you work?	O-tsutome wa dochira desu ka?	お勤めはどちらですか。
When did you join the company?	Nyūsha wa itsu desu ka?	入社はいつですか。
Do you like your work?	O-shigoto wa suki desu ka?	お仕事は好きですか。
What would you like to do?	Nani o shitai n'desu ka?	何をしたいんですか。
I don't work.	Mushoku desu.	無職です。
I'm a/an~.	~ desu/o shite imasu.	～です/をしています。
accountant	kaikeishi	会計士
architect	kenchikuka	建築家
artist	ātisuto, geijutsuka	アーティスト、芸術家
bank employee	ginkōin	銀行員
businessman	bijinesuman	ビジネスマン
clerical worker	jimuin	事務員
company employee	kaishain	会社員
consultant	konsarutanto	コンサルタント
dentist	shikai, ha-isha	歯科医、歯医者
diplomat	gaikōkan	外交官
director/executive	(kaisha) yakuin	(会社) 役員
distributor	ryūtsū gyōsha	流通業者
editor	henshūsha	編集者
engineer	gishi	技師
factory worker	kōin	工員
farmer	nōka	農家
financial businessman	kin'yū gyōsha	金融業者
fisherman	ryōshi	漁師
foreign trader	bōeki gyōsha	貿易業者
government worker	kōmuin	公務員
housewife	shufu	主婦
journalist	jānarisuto	ジャーナリスト
lawyer	bengoshi	弁護士
manufacturer	seizō gyōsha	製造業者

medical doctor	isha	医者
musician	ongakuka	音楽家
professor	daigaku kyōju	大学教授
public official	kōmuin	公務員
secretary	hisho	秘書
shop owner	shōten keieisha	商店経営者
student	gakusei	学生
teacher	kyōshi	教師
translator	hon'yakuka	翻訳家
veterinarian	jūi	獣医
wholesaler	oroshiuri gyōsha	卸売り業者
I'm in the ~ business.	~ o shite imasu.	〜をしています。
agriculture	nōgyō	農業
commerce	shōgyō	商業
construction industry	kensetsugyō	建設業
distribution	ryūtsū kikō	流通機構
finance business	kin'yūgyō	金融業
fishery	gyogyō	漁業
industry/manufacturing	kōgyō/seizōgyō	工業／製造業
service industry	sābisugyō	サービス業
transport business	unsōgyō	運送業

WORK	COMPANY	INDUSTRY	PART-TIME JOB
仕事	会社	産業	アルバイト
shigoto	kaisha	sangyō	arubaito

OCCUPATION	FACTORY	SELF-EMPLOYMENT	RETIREMENT
職業	工場	自営業	退職
shokugyō	kōjō	jieigyō	taishoku

ESSENTIAL VERBS

to work	**to change jobs**	**to quit**
働く	転職する	辞める
hataraku	tenshoku suru	yameru

47

HOME

The cost of housing is astronomical in Japan, particularly in the cities. Along with the children's education, a family's primary cash outlay is for its housing. Single people who can't afford to buy or rent often live with their parents until marriage—and often afterwards—or in company-subsidized dormitories.

One pleasure of visiting a Japanese home is seeing some ingenious methods of making the best of tight spaces. Equally interesting is how Japanese adapt Western things like furniture and ornamentation to suit their own needs and inspirations.

Where is your home?	O-sumai wa dochira desu ka?	お住まいはどちらですか。
Is it in the city or suburbs?	Toshin desu ka soretomo kōgai desu ka?	都心ですかそれとも郊外ですか。
city	toshin	都心
suburbs	kōgai	郊外
countryside	inaka	田舎
What is your home like?	Donna o-taku desu ka?	どんなお宅ですか。
It's a/an ~.	~ desu.	〜です。
big house	ōki-na ie	大きな家
small house	chiisa-na ie	小さな家
wooden house	mokuzō	木造
concrete building	tekkin	鉄筋
apartment	apāto	アパート
condo, apartment bldg	manshon	マンション
high-rise building	kōsō biru	高層ビル
I live alone.	Hitori de sunde imasu.	一人で住んでいます。
I live with my ~.	~ to issho ni sunde imasu.	〜といっしょに住んでいます。
friend	tomodachi	友達
boy/girl friend, lover	koibito	恋人
mother	haha	母
father	chichi	父
wife	tsuma	妻
husband	otto	夫
relatives	shinseki	親戚

FURNISHINGS

WESTERN-STYLE ROOM 洋室 yōshitsu	**DINING ROOM** 食堂 shokudō	**LIVING ROOM** 居間 ima	**RESTROOM** お手洗い o-tearai
BEDROOM 寝室 shinshitsu	**KITCHEN** 台所 daidokoro	**GARAGE** 車庫 shako	**SHOWER** シャワー shawā
JAPANESE-STYLE 和室 washitsu	**TATAMI MAT** 畳 tatami	**ROOM SIZE** *(in mats)* 〜畳間 ~jōma	**JAPANESE BATHTUB** お風呂 o-furo
HOUSE 家 ie	**FUTON** ふとん futon	**DRAWER** 引き出し hikidashi	**WALL** 壁 kabe
ROOM 部屋 heya	**CARPET, RUG** 絨毯 jūtan	**CUPBOARD** 食器棚 shokki dana	**MIRROR** 鏡 kagami
FLOOR PLAN 間取り madori	**TABLE** テーブル tēburu	**WINDOW** 窓 mado	**SHELF** 棚 tana
YOUR RESIDENCE お住まい o-sumai	**DESK** 机 tsukue	**CURTAIN** カーテン kāten	**BOOKSHELF** 本棚 hon dana
FURNITURE 家具 kagu	**CHAIR** 椅子 isu	**DOOR** ドア doa	**FRONT ENTRANCE** 玄関 genkan
BED ベッド beddo	**SOFA** ソファ sofa	**KEY** 鍵 kagi	**GARDEN, YARD** 庭 niwa

SCHOOLING AND EDUCATION

For many Japanese children, education is neither a time of enlightenment nor a passage into adulthood. It is instead an "examination hell," as the Japanese themselves say, focused solely on passing standardized and highly competitive tests for entrance into desired schools, from kindergarten to college. The ultimate goal is entry into one of a select group of universities, which can in turn assure future work in government or business. It is well established, if not explicitly acknowledged, that only a very few universities can open doors into elite careers in public service.

Until they enter the university, many Japanese students have little spare time, whether for play or developing personal interests. At the end of the regular school day, a second shift starts, either with hours of homework, or at one of the ubiquitous private "cram schools" called juku, where rote memorization translates into big business.

Entrance into university is the start of the easy life. Unlike the years through high school, little out-of-class study is required or even expected at Japanese universities. (Japanese students studying at universities overseas are often initially stunned by how much work there is.)

For Japanese schoolchildren, the school year begins in April, with a six-week summer vacation and short vacations over New Year's and at the end of March.

Most students go on organized school trips around November, with seemingly half of the country's students ending up in Kyoto all at once. Should you undertake an autumn excursion to Kyoto, beware . . .

Are you a student?	Gakusei desu ka?	学生ですか。
Do you go to school?	Gakkō e itte iru n'desu ka?	学校へ行っているんですか。
Where do you go to school?	Gakkō wa dochira desu ka?	学校はどちらですか。
When will you graduate?	Itsu go-sotsugyō desu ka?	いつご卒業ですか。
What time does school start?	Gakkō wa nan ji kara desu ka?	学校は何時からですか。
What time does school end?	Gakkō wa nan ji ni owarimasu ka?	学校は何時に終わりますか。
Do you like school?	Gakkō wa suki desu ka?	学校は好きですか。
What are you studying in school?	Gakkō de nani o benkyō shite iru n'desu ka?	学校で何を勉強しているんですか。

What subject do you like?	Suki-na gakka wa nan desu ka?	好きな学科は何ですか。
What do you teach?	Nani o oshiete imasu ka?	何を教えていますか。
What is your field?	Go-senmon wa nan desu ka?	ご専門は何ですか。
I want to study ~.	~ o benkyō shitai desu.	～を勉強したいです。
anthropology	jinruigaku	人類学
biology	seibutsugaku	生物学
chemistry	kagaku	化学
economics	keizaigaku	経済学
engineering	kōgaku	工学
environmental science	kankyō kagaku	環境科学
geography	chirigaku	地理学
geology	chigaku	地学
history	rekishigaku	歴史学
law	hōgaku	法学
mathematics	sūgaku	数学
medicine	igaku	医学
pharmacy	yakugaku	薬学
philosophy	tetsugaku	哲学
physics	butsurigaku	物理学
political science	seijigaku	政治学
psychology	shinrigaku	心理学
science	kagaku	科学
sociology	shakaigaku	社会学
When is your ~?	~ wa itsu desu ka?	～はいつですか。
summer vacation	natsu yasumi	夏休み
winter vacation	fuyu yasumi	冬休み

SCHOOL 学校 gakkō	**ELEMENTARY SCHOOL** 小学校 shōgakkō	**UNIVERSITY** 大学 daigaku	**TEACHER, INSTRUCTOR** 先生 sensei
NURSERY SCHOOL 保育園 hoikuen	**JUNIOR HIGH SCHOOL** 中学校 chūgakkō	**GRADUATE SCHOOL** 大学院 daigakuin	**STUDIES** 勉強、学問 benkyō, gakumon
KINDERGARDEN 幼稚園 yōchien	**HIGH SCHOOL** 高校、高等学校 kōkō, kōtō gakkō	**STUDENT** 学生 gakusei	**AREA OF STUDY** 専攻、専門 senkō, senmon

Utilities

UTILITIES

TELEPHONE AND INTERNET

Public phones are becoming less common since *keitai*, or cell phones, are so common in Japan. Public phones can generally be found at hotels, train stations, outside many convenience stores, and other public areas. They sport a variety of colors, and offer a variety of capabilities. Most common and useful are the vibrant green phones. Insert a few ¥10 coins and dial. When an obnoxious beep intrudes, put in more coins immediately, or quickly say *sayōnara*.

Most green phones can be used only for domestic calls. Green phones generally accept either prepaid phone cards or coins. Prepaid cards are handy and often feature interesting photos or artwork. The cards, which come in various denominations, are available from station kiosks and many convenience stores.

International calls can be made only from specially-designated public phones. Gray phones are mostly likely to offer international direct dialing. When making such a call, dial 001 + the country code and then the desired number. Dark gray phones, available in airports and some hotel lobbies, accept phone cards and provide jacks for laptop computers. Old-fashioned pink phones may still be found in some coffee shops. They accept only ¥10 coins and can be used only for local calls.

Some foreign cell phones can be used in Japan. Check with your provider before traveling. It is also possible to rent a cell phone. You can reserve a cell phone in advance and pick it up at the airport upon your arrival. Once you are in Japan, you can also arrange to have one delivered to your accomodation.

If you plan to bring your laptop, first check that it is compatible with Japan's unique electric current (100 V AC, 60 Hz in western Japan, 50 Hz in eastern Japan.) Most laptops can be used without difficulty. However, you'll need either a plug adaptor or transformer to fit your 3-pronged plug into Japan's two-pin wall sockets. Phone jacks in Japan are compatible with those used in the U.S.

Most modern hotels have internet service. In general, internet service is available in your room if you bring your own laptop, but in some cases wireless service may be offered in the lobby or other designated area. Internet cafés are common in major cities, and many coffee shops offer wireless service for customers. *Manga kissa* (24-hour comic book reading rooms) offer internet service as well as ample reading material and, in many cases, cheap accomodations.

TELEPHONE

Where is a public telephone?	Kōshū denwa wa doko desu ka?	公衆電話はどこですか。
May I use your phone?	Denwa o o-kari dekimasu ka?	電話をお借りできますか。
I'd like to make a local call.	Shinai denwa o kaketai n'desu ga.	市内電話をかけたいんですが。
Is there an English directory?	Eigo no denwachō ga arimasu ka?	英語の電話帳がありますか。
I'll pay for it here.	Ryōkin wa watashi ga haraimasu.	料金は私が払います。
This is an emergency.	Kinkyū desu.	緊急です。

I'd like extension ~.	Naisen ~ o onegai shimasu.	内線～をお願いします。
I'd like room service.	Rūmu sābisu o onegai shimasu.	ルームサービスをお願いします。
I'd like the front desk.	Furonto o onegai shimasu.	フロントをお願いします。
I'd like the number for ~.	~ no denwa bangō o onegai shimasu.	～の電話番号をお願いします。
I'd like to call ~.	~ e denwa shitai n'desu ga.	～へ電話をしたいんですが。
I'd like to make a/an ~ call.	~ o onegai shimasu.	～をお願いします。
collect	korekuto kōru	コレクトコール
credit card	kurejitto kādo kōru	クレジットカードコール
international	kokusai denwa	国際電話
domestic long-distance	chōkyori denwa	長距離電話

Hello?	Moshi-moshi.	もしもし。
Hello, is this ~?	Moshi-moshi. ~-san desu ka?	もしもし。～さんですか。
May I speak to ~?	~-san o onegai shimasu.	～さんをお願いします。
Is ~ there?	~-san wa irasshaimasu ka?	～さんはいらっしゃいますか。
I'd like extension ~.	Naisen no ~ o onegai shimasu.	内線の～をお願いします。
This is ~.	~ desu.	～です。
May I speak in English?	Eigo de hanashite ii desu ka?	英語で話していいですか。
Please give me someone who speaks English.	Eigo no hanaseru hito o onegai shimasu.	英語の話せる人をお願いします。
Sorry, I don't understand anything.	Sumimasen ga zenzen wakarimasen.	すみませんが全然わかりません。
I don't speak Japanese.	Nihongo o hanasemasen.	日本語を話せません。
My telephone number here is ~.	Watashi no denwa bangō wa ~ ban desu.	私の電話番号は～番です。
I'll call again later.	Mata ato de denwa shimasu.	また後で電話します。

WEATHER

The Japanese dwell on the weather, savoring every small change and nuance with nearly pathological enthusiasm. Newspapers and television trumpet in all earnestness that the rainy season arrived two days later than normal, or that spring's first cherry blossom was sighted. On a slow news day, the weather can be the lead story. Seasonal nuances make perfect small talk—for hours.

There are indeed four seasons in most of Japan. Except to the north in Hokkaido, and the mountains of Honshu, summers are hot and often muggy. Come autumn, typhoon season hits Japan, along with most of the rest of Asia. Most typhoons lose much of their energy over the Philippines and Taiwan before eventually hitting Japan, usually in the south around Kyushu and Shikoku. Nevertheless, one or two typhoons—identified by numbers, not names—usually pack a substantial wallop. Winter is cool in the south, cold in the north, with the western side taking the brunt of Siberian storms carrying moisture from the Sea of Japan. Spring is brief, as is cherry blossom season. A short rainy season from mid-June to mid-July, called *tsuyu*, precedes summer's heat.

When it rains, however light and benign, everyone sprouts an umbrella. If you get caught without one, convenience stores carry cheap disposable ones. In fact, umbrellas are probably one of Japan's biggest bargains.

It's a nice day, isn't it?	Kyō wa ii tenki desu ne.	今日はいい天気ですね。
It's bad weather, isn't it?	Kyō wa iya-na tenki desu ne.	今日はいやな天気ですね。
It's hot today, isn't it?	Kyō wa atsui desu ne.	今日は暑いですね。
It's cold today, isn't it?	Kyō wa samui desu ne.	今日は寒いですね。
What is ~ forecast?	~ tenki yohō wa dō desu ka?	~天気予報はどうですか。
today's	Kyō no	今日の
tonight's	Kon'ya no	今夜の
tomorrow's	Ashita no	明日の

WEATHER	FORECAST	AIR TEMPERATURE	LIKELIHOOD OF RAIN
天気	天気予報	気温	降水確率
tenki	tenki yohō	kion	kōsui kakuritsu

The weather will probably be ~. 天気は～でしょう。		There will probably be ~. おそらく～となるでしょう。		

HOT 暑い atsui	WARM 暖かい atatakai	FINE WEATHER 晴れ hare	CLOUDY 曇り kumori	COMFORT-ABLE 快適 kaiteki
COLD 寒い samui	COOL 涼しい suzushii	MUGGY 蒸し暑い mushiatsui	WINDY 風が強い kaze ga tsuyoi	UNCOMFORT-ABLE 不快 fukai

SUNSHINE 日光 nikkō	SHOWER にわか雨 niwaka ame	SNOW 雪 yuki	RAINBOW 虹 niji	LIGHTNING 稲妻 inazuma
CLOUD 雲 kumo	RAINSTORM 嵐 arashi	SNOWSTORM 吹雪 fubuki	FOG, MIST 霧 kiri	TYPHOON 台風 taifū
RAIN 雨 ame	DOWNPOUR 土砂降り doshaburi	WIND 風 kaze	THUNDER 雷 kaminari	FOUR SEASONS 四季 shiki

ESSENTIAL VERBS

to become cloudy 曇る kumoru	to snow 雪が降る yuki ga furu	to be windy 風が吹く kaze ga fuku
to clear up 晴れる hareru	to rain 雨が降る ame ga furu	to become cold, chilly 冷える hieru

LAUNDRY AND DRY CLEANING

There are dry cleaning shops nearly everywhere, most of them pickup and drop-off outlets that send clothes to central cleaning centers.

Coin laundries, or laundromats, are not especially common, nor are places to leave laundry for service washes or drop-off service.

Where is the nearest ~?	Ichiban chikai ~ wa doko desu ka?	一番近い〜はどこですか。
laundry	sentakuya	洗濯屋
dry cleaner	dorai kuriininguya	ドライクリーニング
laundromat	koin randorii	コインランドリー
I have some laundry/dry cleaning.	Sentaku / Kuriiningu o tanomimasu.	洗濯／クリーニングを頼みます。
I'd like this pressed.	Kore ni airon o kakete kudasai.	これにアイロンをかけて下さい。
I'd like this repaired.	Kore o tsukurotte kudasai.	これをつくろって下さい。
Can you send it out?	Dashite oite moraemasu ka?	出しておいてもらえますか。
When will it be ready?	Itsu dekimasu ka?	いつできますか。
Will it be ready by ~?	~ made ni dekimasu ka?	〜までにできますか。
I need it ~.	~hitsuyō na n'desu ga.	〜必要なんですが。
tonight	konban	今晩
tomorrow	ashita	明日
the day after tomorrow	asatte	明後日
My laundry's been damaged.	Sentakumono ga itande imashita.	洗濯物がいたんでいました。
These clothes don't belong to me.	Kore wa watashi no fuku de wa arimasen.	これは私の服ではありません。

SWEATER セーター sētā	**SKIRT** スカート sukāto	**SUIT** スーツ sūtsu	**SLACKS** スラックス surakkusu	**LAUNDRY** 洗濯屋 sentakuya
COAT コート kōto	**BLOUSE** ブラウス burausu	**NECKTIE** ネクタイ nekutai	**UNDERWEAR** 下着 shitagi	**DRY CLEANER** ドライクリーニング屋 dorai kuriininguya
DRESS ワンピース wanpiisu	**SLIP** スリップ surippu	**SHIRT** シャツ shatsu	**SOCKS** 靴下 kutsushita	**LAUNDROMAT** コインランドリー koin randorii

PHOTOGRAPHY

If photography is your interest, Japan is nirvana, heaven, paradise. Everyone has a camera, everyone takes "I've been here" pictures, and almost no one minds having their photograph taken. Japanese understand and cherish the ritual of taking pictures. About the only places that might restrict photography are certain museums, temples, and shrines—there will usually be a sign in English. Film of all kinds is available everywhere, as are processing and printing in every conceivable size. In the countryside, many shops are an agent for processing and printing.

Can I take photos?	Shashin o totte mo ii desu ka?	写真をとってもいいですか。
Can I use the flash?	Furasshu o tsukatte mo ii desu ka?	フラッシュを使ってもいいですか。
Could you please take my photograph for me?	Shashin o totte itadakemasu ka?	写真をとっていただけますか。
Let's have our picture taken together.	Issho ni shashin o totte kudasai.	一緒に写真をとって下さい。
May I take your photograph?	Shashin o torasete itadakemasu ka?	写真をとらせていただけますか。

Color slide film, please.	Suraidoyō karā firumu o kudasai.	スライド用カラーフィルムを下さい。
Color print film, please.	Karā firumu o kudasai.	カラーフィルムを下さい。
A battery, please.	Denchi o kudasai.	電池を下さい。
I'd like this film developed.	Genzō shitai n'desu ga.	現像したいんですが。
I'd like to have this printed.	Yakimashi shitai n'desu ga.	焼き増ししたいんですが。
This camera has a problem.	Kamera no chōshi ga warui n'desu ga.	カメラの調子が悪いんですが。
Can you check it for me?	Chotto mite moraemasu ka?	ちょっと見てもらえますか。
Please fix my camera.	Kamera o shūri shite kudasai.	カメラを修理して下さい。
When will it be ready?	Itsu dekimasu ka?	いつできますか。

PHOTOGRAPH	NO PHOTOGRAPHS	NO FLASH
写真	撮影禁止	フラッシュ禁止
shashin	satsuei kinshi	furasshu kinshi

MONEY

Japan is a land of cash. Japanese prefer cash to credit cards and bank checks, and so often carry huge wads of cash with them. And it's no problem to use a ¥10,000 note for a ¥95 purchase. Merchants always have plenty of change.

Bank checks are in fact nearly nonexistent. Use of credit cards is not prevalent either, although it is becoming increasingly common among the young and upwardly mobile. And although credit cards are gaining a foothold, businesses accepting Visa and MasterCard, for example, may accept only those issued by Japanese banks. Don't be surprised if yours is turned down. Carry lots of cash in case.

genkin
cash

Bank interiors in Japan are typically quiet and serene places, with comfortable and ample seating. There's a good reason for this. Japanese banks are slow and lethargic, with layers of identically uniformed clerks reviewing and approving transactions. A uniformed OL, or office lady, at the front counter takes your money and paperwork and graciously waves you to one of those comfortable seats. When you're needed again, your name will be called out, followed by the honorific suffix *-sama*.

ATMs are common, but many will not accept your foreign credit or debit card. However, there are generally a few international ATMs available in major cities. In additon, you can use your card to obtain cash at ATMs in most large post offices and at 7-eleven convenience stores, which are quite common. Cash machines at banks often charge a higher fee during hours when the bank is not open.

GETTING TO A BANK

Most travelers visit a bank to exchange money. A bank that will exchange foreign currencies will have a sign in English near its door indicating that it's an authorized foreign exchange bank. Alternatively, hotels can cash traveler's checks for registered guests, though exchange rates tend to be lower.

Carry traveler's checks in U.S. dollars or Japanese yen. Plan on cashing them before leaving the cities; in the countryside, you will likely have difficulty using them.

Where is the nearest bank?	Ichiban chikai gjnkō wa doko desu ka?	一番近い銀行はどこですか。
How late is the bank open?	Ginkō wa nan ji made yatte imasu ka?	銀行は何時までやっていますか。
When will it open?	Itsu akimasu ka?	いつ開きますか。
Where can I change money?	Doko de ryōgae dekimasu ka?	どこで両替できますか。
Is there another bank nearby?	Chikaku ni hoka no ginkō ga arimasu ka?	近くに他の銀行がありますか。

BANK	MONEY	COIN	1,000 YEN	CREDIT CARD
銀行	お金	硬貨	千円	クレジットカード
ginkō	o-kane	kōka	sen'en	kurejitto kādo
BRANCH	**CASH**	**BILL**	**10,000 YEN**	**TRAVELER'S CHECK**
支店	現金	お札	一万円	トラベラーズチェック
shiten	genkin	o-satsu	ichi man'en	toraberāzu chekku

DINERS CLUB	MASTERCARD	VISA	AMERICAN EXPRESS
ダイナーズクラブ	マスターカード	ビザ	アメリカンエクスプレス
daināzu kurabu	**masutā kādo**	**biza**	**amerikan ekusupuresu**

EXCHANGING MONEY

What's the exchange rate?	Kawese rēto wa ikura desu ka?	為替レートはいくらですか。
I'd like to change ~ dollars.	~ doru o ryōgae shite kudasai.	～ドルを両替して下さい。
I'd like to change it to yen.	En ni shitai n'desu ga.	円にしたいんですが。
I'd like to cash a traveler's check.	Toraberāzu chekku o genkin ni kaetai n'desu ga.	トラベラーズチェックを現金に替えたいんですが。
Give me large bills, please.	Kogaku shihei o kudasai.	高額紙幣を下さい。
Give me small bills, please.	Shōgaku shihei o kudasai.	小額紙幣を下さい。
Can you cash a traveler's check in ~?	Toraberāzu chekku o ~ ni shite moraemasu ka?	トラベラーズチェックを～にしてもらえますか。
Can you change ~ to yen?	~ o en ni kaete moraemasu ka?	～を円に替えてもらえますか。
Change this to ~, please.	~ ni kōkan shite kudasai.	～に交換して下さい。

FOREIGN EXCHANGE 外国為替 gaikoku kawase	SINGAPORE $ シンガポールドル shingapōru doru	EURO ユーロ yūro	CANADIAN $ カナダドル kanada doru
EXCHANGE RATE 為替レート kawase rēto	HONGKONG $ 香港ドル honkon doru	NEW ZEALAND $ ニュージーランドドル nyū jiirando doru	AUSTRALIAN $ オーストラリアドル ōsutoraria doru
US $ ドル doru	BRITISH POUND ポンド pondo		

No, we can't. いいえ、できません。	The ~ bank probably can. ～銀行ならできるでしょう。
Yes, we can. はい、できます。	I don't know who can exchange it. どこで両替できるかわかりません。
... but it'll take a few days. でも2、3日かかります。	It's difficult to do outside of Tokyo/Osaka. 東京／大阪以外では難しいです。

TRANSFERRING MONEY

International transfers of money should be attempted only at large urban bank branches. Whatever the reason—and the excuses often sound dubious—smaller branches will frequently say they can't make transfers. Most large branches have money transfer applications in English and Japanese. If your request seems to have flustered the staff, best to find another bank.

It's possible to send money to postal accounts in other countries. All delivery post offices offer international postal remittance (*kokusai sōkin*). For visitors whose home countries have postal savings systems, money transfers can be made directly to home-country postal giro accounts at very economical rates, cheaper than through banks or via mail.

I'd like a ~.	~ o onegai shimasu.	〜をお願いします。
mail transfer application	gaikokumuke futsū sōkin iraisho	外国向普通送金 (M/T) 依頼書
demand draft application	sōkin kogitte sakusei iraisho	送金小切手 (D/D) 作成依頼書
wire transfer application	gaikokumuke denshin sōkin iraisho	外国向電信送金 (T//T) 依頼書
I'd like to transfer money to the ~ bank, ～ branch.	~ ginkō ～~ shiten ni furikomitai n'desu ga.	〜銀行〜〜支店に振り込みたいんですが。
How long will it take?	Dono kurai kakarimasu ka?	どのくらいかかりますか。

MONEY TRANSFER	WIRE TRANSFER	BRANCH NAME	SENDER'S NAME
振込	電信送金	支店名	ご依頼人
furikomi	denshin sōkin	shitenmei	go-irainin
REMITTANCE 送金 sōkin	**OVERSEAS TRANSFER** 外国送金 gaikoku sōkin	**RECIPIENT'S NAME** お受取人 o-uketorinin	**DATE OF REQUEST** ご依頼日 go-iraibi
DEMAND DRAFT 送金小切手 (D/D) sōkin kogitte (D/D)	**DESTINATION BANK** 先方銀行 senpō ginkō	**RECIPIENT'S BANK** 支払銀行 shiharai ginkō	**TRANSFER AMOUNT** 送金金額 sōkin kingaku
MAIL TRANSFER 郵便振替 yūbin furikae	**BANK NAME** 銀行名 ginkōmei	**RECIPIENT'S ACCOUNT #** 受取人口座番号 uketori-nin kōza bangō	**NAME** 氏名 shimei

MAIL

Domestic mail service in Japan is excellent and predictably conscientious. It is also relatively expensive, as is international mail. A postcard from Hong Kong to Tokyo is half the price of one from Tokyo to Tokyo.

Mail for domestic delivery, whether mailed from overseas or within Japan, can be addressed in roman letters. Be sure to print the name and address, rather than writing them in cursive.

International parcels require a special shipping label, which is in both Japanese and English. You'll be handed one when you try to send your package.

yūbin
postal service

There is an efficient and economical international express mail service—EMS—but with an odd quirk. It's considered to be for business use and technically one requires an account number. Most clerks don't care if you have an account, but they need a number written in the box. As a result, some people have been known to fake it by writing "D/j 160-545," or something like that. (160 is a postal code, 545 the account number.)

Postal savings is big business and gives the government a large source of capital for investment and spending. Visitors from countries with postal savings can make international money transfers from most post offices in Japan.

ORIENTATION

Standard domestic services, including registered mail and special delivery delivered by motorcycle couriers nearly anywhere in Japan by the next day, are available in all post offices. It's also possible to send large amounts of cash domestically by registered mail, using special security envelopes sold for a few yen.

Post offices keep decent hours, including Saturdays, and are easy to find. (For about the same number of post offices nationwide, Japan's postal system handles just one-eighth the volume of mail in America.) Inside almost every post office are two sets of signs: green and red. Head for a counter with red signs, which indicate mailing windows. The green signs are for postal banking windows.

Where Is the post office?	Yūbin kyoku wa doko desu ka?	郵便局はどこですか。
Is it open now?	Ima aite imasu ka?	今開いていますか。
Where's a mail box?	Posuto wa doko desu ka?	ポストはどこですか。
What window should I go to for stamps?	Kitte wa dono madoguchi desu ka?	切手はどの窓口ですか。
Where's the general delivery window?	Kyokudome yūbin no mado-guchi wa doko desu ka?	局留郵便の窓口はどこですか。
Is there any mail for me?	Watashi ate ni yūbin ga kite imasu ka?	私宛に郵便が来ていますか。

ESSENTIAL VERBS

to write a letter
手紙を書く
tegami o kaku

to insure a parcel
保険をかける
hoken o kakeru

to deliver
配達する
haitatsu suru

to send a letter
手紙を出す
tegami o dasu

to send
送る
okuru

to reach
届く
todoku

to send a parcel
小包を送る
kozutsumi o okuru

to send, have delivered
届ける
todokeru

to receive
受け取る
uketoru

SENDING

The postal clerk may seem rather nosy about exactly what's inside your package. Usually he's trying to find out if there's a letter inside, which makes the package more expensive to send, or if there's a book, which can be sent much more cheaply as long as there's no letter enclosed with it. When you send a book, the clerk will suggest that the corner of the package be snipped off for inspection, which is probably what his confusing gestures are all about.

Would you take care of this?	Onegai shimasu.	お願いします。
I want to send this by the cheapest way.	Kore o ichiban yasui hōhō de okuritai n'desu ga.	これを一番安い方法で送りたいんですが。
I want to send this by the fastest way.	Kore o ichiban hayai hōhō de okuritai n'desu ga.	これを一番速い方法で送りたいんですが。
How much is the postage for this?	Kore wa ikura desu ka?	これはいくらですか。
How much is it to send this by ~?	~ de ikura desu ka?	～でいくらですか。
Please send this by ~.	~ de onegai shimasu.	～でお願いします。
airmail	kōkūbin	航空便
registered mail	kakitome	書留
special delivery	sokutatsu	速達
EMS (int'l express mail)	kokusai ekusupuresu mēru	国際エクスプレスメール (EMS)
air parcel	kōkū kozutsumi	航空小包
SAL (sea/air) parcel	saru kozutsumi	SAL小包
surface parcel	funabin kozutsumi	船便小包
recorded delivery	kan'i kakitome	簡易書留
COD/cash on delivery	chakubarai	着払い
forwarding	tensō	転送
insured	hoken tsuki	保険付
small packet	kogata hōsōbutsu	小型包装物
printed matter	insatsubutsu	印刷物
book rate	shoseki kozutsumi	書籍小包
Please insure this.	Hoken o kakete kudasai.	保険をかけて下さい。
How long will it take to reach ~?	Nan nichi de ~ e tsukimasu ka?	何日で～へ着きますか。

STAMPS AND STUFF

~ ~~ -yen stamps, please.	~ ~ en kitte o ~ -mai kudasai.	〜〜円切手を〜枚下さい。
I want to buy a/an ~.	~ o kaitai n'desu ga.	〜を買いたいんですが。
postage stamp	kitte	切手
aerogram	kōkū shokan	航空書簡
commemorative stamp	kinen kitte	記念切手
envelope	fūtō	封筒
international money order	kokusai yūbin kawase	国際郵便為替
international reply coupon	kokusai henshin kitteken	国際返信切手券
post card	hagaki	はがき
postal money order	yūbin kawase	郵便為替

You can't send it by ~.
〜では送れません。

If there's a letter, it's more expensive.
手紙が入っているともっと高くなります。

We don't sell ~ in this post office.
ここでは〜は売っていません。

We don't have ~ in this post office.
ここには〜はありません。

You'll have to use the central post office (for that service).
中央郵便局でお願いします。

What's inside?
中身はなんですか。

If there's a letter, it's more expensive.
手紙が入っているともっと高くなります。

I must look inside.
中身を調べなくてはなりません。

You'll have to wrap this stronger.
もっとしっかり包装しなくてはいけません。

It's cheaper if I cut open the corner of the envelope for inspection.
ふうとうの隅を切っておけば安くなります。

LETTER	BOOK	GIFT	PHOTOGRAPH	SOUVENIR
手紙	本	プレゼント	写真	おみやげ
tegami	hon	purezento	shashin	o-miyage

UTILITIES

POST OFFICE	FORWARDING	NIGHT WINDOW	TOKYO AREA
郵便局 yūbin kyoku	転送 tensō	夜間受付窓口 yakan uketsuke madoguchi	東京都 Tōkyō-to
POSTAL SERVICES 郵便 yūbin	LETTER 手紙 tegami	MAILBOX 郵便受け yūbinuke	WEEKDAY PICKUPS 平日集配 heijitsu shūhai
INTERNATIONAL MAIL 国際郵便 kokusai yūbin	POSTAGE 郵便料金 yūbin ryōkin	MAILBOX ポスト posuto	SUNDAY, HOLIDAYS 休日 kyūjitsu
PACKAGE, PARCEL 小包 kozutsumi	MAIL DELIVERY 郵便配達 yūbin haitatsu	LOCAL 市内 shinai	OUT-OF-TOWN, OTHER その他の地域 sono ta no chiiki

FILLING OUT FORMS

Increasingly, forms for international mailings and money trans-actions are available in both Japanese and English. If not, the application form labels below should help out. Print in block letters, like in your kindergarten days. Clear, simple, and minus your personal flourishes—helps ensure no mistakes. Note also that it's possible to have luggage delivered between main airports and one's destination, and between any two points in Japan by private delivery service. The forms for these delivery services are usually only in Japanese.

TO	SENDER	ADDRESS	DATE MAILED
お届け先 o-todokesaki	発信人 hasshinnin	住所 jūsho	差出年月日 sashidashi nengappi
FROM ご依頼主 go-irainushi	NAME/ADDRESS 宛名 atena	FULL NAME 氏名 shimei	POSTAL CODE 郵便番号 yūbin bangō
ADDRESSEE 受信人 jushinnin	ADDRESS 宛先 atesaki	NAME 名前 namae	CONTENTS 内容 naiyō

PUBLIC SIGNS AND NOTICES

SIGNS 掲示 keiji	**ESCALATORS** エスカレーター esukarētā	**NO SMOKING** 禁煙 kin'en	**DO NOT USE** 使用禁止 shiyō kinshi
CLOSED TODAY 本日休業 honjitsu kyūgyō	**ELEVATORS** エレベーター erebētā	**RESERVED** 貸切 kashikiri	**-PROHIBITED** 〜禁止 ~kinshi
CLOSED 準備中 junbichū	**FOR SALE** 売り物 urimono	**TRASH** ゴミ箱 gomi bako	**KEEP OUT** 立入禁止 tachiiri kinshi
OPEN 営業中 eigyōchū	**DISCOUNT** 割引 waribiki	**OUT OF ORDER** 故障 koshō	**NO TRESPASSING** 進入禁止 shinnyū kinshi
OCCUPIED 使用中 shiyōchū	**INFORMATION** 案内 annai	**WET PAINT** ペンキ塗りたて penki nuritate	**NO PHOTOS** 撮影禁止 satsuei kinshi
EMERGENCY EXIT 非常口 hijō guchi	**INFORMATION DESK** 案内所 annaijo	**EMERGENCY BUTTON** 非常呼出 hijō yobidashi	**NO CROSSING** 横断禁止 ōdan kinshi
ENTRANCE 入口 iriguchi	**RECEPTION DESK** 受付 uketsuke	**WARNING** 警告 keikoku	**NO CROSSING** わたるな wataru na
EXIT 出口 deguchi	**PULL** 引く hiku	**CAUTION** 注意 chūi	**NO PARKING** 駐車禁止 chūsha kinshi
AUTOMATIC DOORS 自動ドア jidōdoa	**PUSH** 押す osu	**DANGER** 危険 kiken	**STOP** 止まれ tomare

GETTING AROUND

Getting Around
WHERE?

Your taxi driver looks disturbingly lost, despite your having given him an address written in Japanese. He's checked a detailed map, queried several pedestrians, and even stopped at the local police box, or *koban*, to get a final, authoritative word. Is he trying to run up the meter on you? No, he's simply lost—but that doesn't mean he's incompetent.

Not only are urban streets often convoluted and thoroughly unsystematic, but most streets and roads in Japan lack names at all, and buildings lack unique street numbers. The address you've supplied simply puts the taxi driver in the right neighborhood. Beyond that, nailing down the destination is a process of narrowing down a list of possibilities, from larger to smaller: prefecture, city, ward, district, neighborhood. So as the taxi winds through Tokyo's labyrinthine back alleys, pity the driver. He would rather your destination were in a large building with a name—Mori Building 644, for example—or a hotel that's on the map.

Other than a lack of clearcut addresses, figuring out directions and locations is no different in Japan than elsewhere. If you can't figure out where you are, and if others you ask are equally in a vacuum, there's always a "police box" in the neighborhood. They usually know where *everything* is, no matter how obscure, and have maps indicating the most insignificant building, identified by number or family or business name. And always try to have your destination written in Japanese. It'll illuminate the way eventually.

Doko?
Where?

WHERE'S THE ADDRESS?

Finding an address is challenging, as named streets and numbered buildings are rare; not even a written address guarantees an easy find. If your destination is written in Japanese, there are probably some hyphenated numbers followed by some Chinese characters—1-4-28 XXX—in the address. Look at a nearby utility pole: there's probably a vertical sign of about a meter's length fixed to its side. Most of the sign is advertising, but at the bottom are usually hyphenated numbers and Chinese characters, hopefully similar to those in your address.

INSIDE AN ADDRESS

Administratively, Japan is divided into 47 main administrative units: one *to* (Tokyo), two *fu* (Osaka, Kyōto), one *dō* (Hokkaido), and 43 *ken*, or prefectures. Instead of street names and numbers, an address focuses in on zones-within-zones, bigger to smaller, from prefectures to increasingly smaller units. Variations abound. It's confusing sometimes.

ADDRESS

住所

jusho

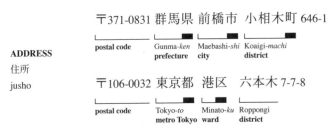

ESSENTIAL VERBS

to go	**to be lost**	**to guide, show**
行く	迷う	案内する
iku	mayou	annai suru
to return home	**to search, look for**	**to turn, curve**
帰る	探す	曲がる
kaeru	sagasu	magaru

ORIENTATION

The Japanese archipelago, or *Nihon rettō*, consists of four main islands and over 3,900 smaller islands extending to Okinawa, near Taiwan. Honshu is the largest island, home to Mt. Fuji, Tokyo, and Kyoto, as well as most bullet train lines. It is also the site of most earthquakes. The northernmost main island, sparsely-populated Hokkaido, is regarded by many Japanese as a romantic rural outback, and it is popular for skiing and honeymoons. Kyushu was Japan's cultural connection to the outside world in ancient times, its proximity to Korea making it Japan's conduit for cultural influence from the Asian mainland. Shikoku is the smallest of the four islands, off the beaten path even for most Japanese. Typhoons hit it regularly.

WORLD	COUNTRY	PREFECTURE	CITY	VILLAGE
世界	国	県	市	村
sekai	kuni	ken	shi	mura
CONTINENT	STATE/ PROVINCE	CAPITAL	TOWN	CITY WARD
大陸	州	首都	町	区
tairiku	shū	shuto	machi	ku

LAND	MOUNTAIN	ASIA	PACIFIC OCEAN	OVERSEAS
陸	山	アジア	太平洋	国外
riku	yama	ajia	taiheiyō	kokugai
ISLAND	SEA, OCEAN	JAPAN	SEA OF JAPAN	REGION
島	海	日本	日本海	地方
shima	umi	Nihon/Nippon	Nihonkai	chihō

INTERNATIONAL	EQUATOR	LATITUDE	NORTH POLE	NO. HEMISPHERE
国際	赤道	緯度	北極	北半球
kokusai	sekidō	ido	hokkyoku	kita hankyū
DOMESTIC	INT'L DATE LINE	LONGITUDE	SOUTH POLE	SO. HEMISPHERE
国内	日付変更線	経度	南極	南半球
kokunai	hizuke henkōsen	keido	nankyoku	minami hankyū

MAP OF JAPAN

Area: 377,873 sq.km.
Population: 127.8 million
Population density: 337 people/sq.km.
Average lifespan: male, 79; female, 86
Per capita GDP: $38,340 (2007)

Japan is divided up into 43 prefectures,
outlined in the map, which are governing
units somewhat like states in the United
States. A larger map is shown on pp. 4-5.

WHERE IS IT?

Edging up to a stranger and flinging out a query in heavily-accented Japanese—and it can truly sound like a foreign language to many Japanese—can result in glazed, if not terrified, looks. When approaching a stranger, politely announce your impending request or question with *Sumimasen ga…*, trailing off in a gentle, humble style. The basic sentence structure for asking about a location or something's (or someone's) whereabouts is: (person/place/thing) *wa doko desu ka?* Using *dochira* instead of doko is even more polite.

Excuse me.	Sumimasen ga…	すみませんが。
I'm looking for ~.	~ o sagashite imasu .	~を探しています。
How do I get to ~?	~ e iku michi o oshiete kudasai.	~へ行く道を教えて下さい。
Where is the ~?	~ wa doko desu ka?	~はどこですか。
Do you know where ~ is?	~ wa doko ka wakarimasu ka?	~はどこか分かりますか。
I can't find the ~.	~ o mitsukeru koto ga deki-masen.	~を見つけることができません。
Is the ~ far from here?	~ wa koko kara tōi desu ka?	~はここから遠いですか。
Is the ~ close to here?	~ wa koko kara chikai desu ka?	~はここから近いですか。
Is there a ~ nearby?	Kono chikaku ni ~ ga arimasu ka?	この近くに~がありますか。
Where is the closest ~ ?	Ichiban chikai ~ wa doko desu ka?	一番近い~はどこですか。
Where is the nearest ~ ?	Moyori no ~ wa doko desu ka?	最寄りの~はどこですか。
How should I get to ~?	~ e wa dō ikeba ii desu ka?	~へはどう行けばいいですか。
I'm trying to get to ~.	~ e ikitai n'desu ga.	~へ行きたいんですが。
I'm looking for ~.	~ o sagashite imasu.	~を探しています。
Which way is ~?	~ wa dochira desu ka?	~はどちらですか。
Where is the road to ~?	~ e iku michi o oshiete kudasai.	~へ行く道を教えて下さい。
Is this the way to ~?	~ e iku michi wa kore de ii desu ka?	~へ行く道はこれでいいですか。
Is this (the) ~?	Koko wa ~ desu ka?	ここは~ですか。
Can someone here speak English?	Eigo o hanaseru hito wa imasu ka?	英語を話せる人はいますか。

It's supposed to be nearby.	Kono chikaku ni aru hazu desu ga.	この近くにあるはずですが。
I'm completely lost.	Kanzen ni mayotte shimaimashita.	完全に迷ってしまいました。
Where are we?	Koko wa doko desu ka?	ここはどこですか。

| POLICE BOX/ STATION 交番 kōban | BANK 銀行 ginkō | SUBWAY STATION 地下鉄の駅 chikatetsu no eki | TOILET/ RESTROOM トイレ toire |
| HOSPITAL 病院 byōin | POST OFFICE 郵便局 yūbin kyoku | TRAIN STATION 駅 eki | PUBLIC TELEPHONE 公衆電話 kōshū denwa |

| BUILDING 建物 tatemono | ENTRANCE 入口 iriguchi | INFORMATION DESK 案内所 annaijo | CASHIER レジ reji |
| ELEVATOR エレベーター erebētā | EXIT 出口 deguchi | LOST AND FOUND 遺失物係 ishitsubutsu gakari | TICKET OFFICE 切符売り場 kippu uriba |

(THIS) HOTEL (この) ホテル (kono) hoteru	BUS STOP バス停 basutei	EMBASSY 大使館 taishikan	OFFICE BUILDING ビル biru
AIRPORT 空港 kūkō	CASTLE 城 shiro	FESTIVAL 祭 matsuri	PARK 公園 kōen
ART GALLERY 画廊 garō	CITY CENTER 市の中心 shi no chushin	LIBRARY 図書館 toshokan	PARKING LOT 駐車場 chūshajō
BOOKSTORE 本屋 hon'ya	CITY OFFICES 市庁舎 shichōsha	MOVIE THEATER 映画館 eigakan	RESTAURANT レストラン resutoran
BRIDGE 橋 hashi	DEPARTMENT STORE デパート depāto	MUSEUM 博物館 hakubutsukan	SHRINE 神社 jinja

NAVIGATING THE STREETS

Maps are lifesavers, especially when written in both Japanese and English. If planning some serious explorations, buy one or even a bilingual atlas. Use it with abandon. Make a habit of learning the kanji for your destination, whether it be a train station, town, or landmark. Study the street layout before bounding out into the confusion.

How long does it take?	Dono kurai kakarimasu ka?	どのくらいかかりますか。
Is it near here?	Sore wa koko kara chikai desu ka?	それはここから近いですか。
Is it far from here?	Sore wa koko kara tōi desu ka?	それはここから遠いですか。
Can I walk there?	Soko e wa aruite ikemasu ka?	そこへは歩いて行けますか。
Can I take a taxi there?	Soko e wa takushii de ikemasu ka?	そこへはタクシーで行けますか。
Can I take a train/subway?	Soko e wa densha de ikemasu ka?	そこへは電車で行けますか。
Which (train) line?	Nan sen desu ka?	何線ですか。
Where do I get off?	Doko no eki de orireba ii desu ka?	どこの駅で降りればいいですか。
What is this street?	Kono tōri wa nan to iimasu ka?	この通りはなんといいますか。
Where are we right now?	Koko wa doko desu ka?	ここはどこですか。
Should I go ~?	~ ni ikeba ii desu ka?	～に行けばいいですか。
straight	massugu	まっすぐ
left	hidari	左
right	migi	右
Please write it here.	Koko ni kaite kudasai.	ここに書いて下さい。
Please write it in Japanese.	Sore o Nihongo de kaite kudasai.	それを日本語で書いて下さい。
Please write it in romaji.	Sore o rōmaji de kaite kudasai.	それをローマ字で書いて下さい。
What does this mean?	Kore wa nan no imi desu ka?	これは何の意味ですか。
Where on this map am I?	Genzaichi o shimeshite kudasai.	現在地を示して下さい。
Please draw me a map here.	Koko ni ryakuzu o kaite kudasai.	ここに略図を書いて下さい。
Do you have maps of the area?	Kono shūhen no chizu wa arimasu ka?	この周辺の地図はありますか。
Which way is ~?	~ wa dochira desu ka?	～はどちらですか。
north	kita	北
south	minami	南

east	higashi	東
west	nishi	西
Are there any land-marks along the way?	Nanika mejirushi ni naru mono ga arimasu ka?	何か目印になるものがありますか。
What is this building?	Kono tatemono wa nan desu ka?	この建物は何ですか。
What is that building?	Ano tatemono wa nan desu ka?	あの建物は何ですか。
Is this the (right) building?	Kono tatemono desu ka?	この建物ですか。
Which building is it?	Dono tatemono desu ka?	どの建物ですか。
Which side is It?	Dochiragawa desu ka?	どちら側ですか。
Which floor is it?	Nan kai desu ka?	何階ですか。
Is it open today?	Kyō wa yatte imasu ka?	今日はやっていますか。
Is it closed all day today?	Kyō wa ichi nichi jū yasumi desu ka?	今日は一日中休みですか。
What time does it open?	Nan ji ni akimasu ka?	何時に開きますか。
What time does it close?	Nan ji ni shimarimasu ka?	何時に閉まりますか。
Whom should I ask?	Dare ni kikeba ii desu ka?	誰に聞けばいいですか。

I have no idea.
全然分かりません。

There's one near here.
この近くにあります。

It's difficult to find.
見つけにくいです。

There isn't one near here.
この近くにはありません。

It's easy to find.
見つけやすいです。

I'll show you where.
私が教えます。

It's not near here.
この辺にはありません。

Please wait here.
ここで待っていて下さい。

You should go ~.
～に行って下さい。

At the ~ turn left/right.
～を左／右へ曲がって下さい。

straight
まっすぐ

It's on the opposite side of the ~.
～の向こうです。

left
左

It's near the ~.
～の近くにあります。

right
右

It's in front of ~.
～の前にあります。

LOCATION AND DIRECTION

LOCATION 位置 ichi	**AHEAD** 先 saki	**IN FRONT OF** 前 mae	**ABOVE, UP, ON** 上 ue	**INDOORS** 内 uchi
DIRECTION 方向 hōkō	**NEXT TO** 隣 tonari	**IN BACK OF** 後 ushiro	**DOWN, UNDER** 下 shita	**OUTDOORS** 外 soto

THIS SIDE こちら側 kochiragawa	**RIGHT SIDE** 右側 migigawa	**LEFT SIDE** 左側 hidarigawa	**BOTH SIDES** 両側 ryōgawa	**OPPOSITE SIDE** 向こう側 mukōgawa

RIGHT 右 migi	**STRAIGHT** まっすぐ massugu	**MIDDLE** 真ん中 mannaka	**OPPOSITE** 向かい mukai	**THE NEXT ~** 次の~ tsugi no ~
LEFT 左 hidari	**BOTH WAYS** 左右 sayū	**INSIDE, CENTER** 中 naka	**OVER THERE** 向こう mukō	**JUST BEFORE ~** ~の手前 ~ no temae

ALLEY, LANE 路地 roji	**AVENUE** 大通り ōdōri	**HIGHWAY** 高速道路 kōsoku dōro	**ROAD, STREET** 道路 dōro	**ROAD, ROUTE** 道 michi

TRAFFIC SIGNAL 信号 shingō	**INTERSECTION** 交差点 kōsaten	**CROSSROADS** 十字路 jūjiro	**SIDEWALK** 歩道 hodō	**DETOUR** 回り道 mawarimichi
CORNER 角 kado	**T-INTERSECTION** つきあたり tsukiatari	**TRAIN CROSSING** 踏切 fumikiri	**DEAD END** 行き止まり ikidomari	**SHORT CUT** 近道 chikamichi

GEOGRAPHICAL LANDMARKS

Geographical landmarks tend to become tourist destinations in themselves—a westernmost cape is visited because it is the westernmost cape, not necessarily because it's especially pretty. Peninsulas, islands, hills, and waterfalls can become landmarks—"famous," as it's often translated in English—for local people.

GEOGRAPHY 地理 chiri	DESERT 砂漠 sabaku	ISLAND 島 shima	MOUNTAIN 山 yama	RAVINE 渓谷 keikoku
BASIN 盆地 bonchi	FOREST 森 mori	LAND 陸 riku	MOUNTAIN RANGE 山脈 sanmyaku	SLOPE, INCLINE 坂 saka
CAPE 岬 misaki	FOREST, WOODS 森林 shinrin	LEVEL GROUND 平地 heichi	MOUNTAIN SUMMIT 頂上 chōjō	VALLEY 谷 tani
COAST 海岸 kaigan	HILL 丘 oka	MARSH 沼 numa	PENINSULA 半島 hantō	VOLCANO 火山 kazan
BAY, GULF 湾 wan	HOT SPRINGS 温泉 onsen	POND 池 ike	SEA, OCEAN 海 umi	STRAITS 海峡 kaikyō
HARBOR 港 minato	LAKE 湖 mizu'umi	RIVER 川 kawa	SEASHORE 海岸 kaigan	WATERFALL 滝 taki
COUNTRY 国 kuni	STATE, PROVINCE 州 shū	CITY 市 shi	TOWN 町 machi	VILLAGE 村 mura

旅

行

ryokō
travel

TRAVEL

Travel in Japan can be both enchanting and confounding. A day's delightful wanderings can come to a sour conclusion when you're turned away from a cozy-looking hotel or inn not because it's full, but because you're a foreigner. It happens occasionally outside of urban areas, and there's nothing you can do except move on down the road. Often, the host's reason for refusal stems from his fear of cultural and language barriers.

There's no denying that travel in Japan is expensive. But travel expenses can be tempered by staying at hostels, using rail passes, taking local buses, and eating working-class noodles and rice balls.

Carry lots of cash, especially outside of large cities. In much of Japan, traveler's checks are not widely accepted, and foreign credit cards may not be accepted either. Don't worry about carrying so much cash—barring absent-minded folly on your part, it should be quite safe, just like you.

Organized tourism is a juggernaut in Japan, highly developed and ubiquitous. Regardless of where one seeks refuge, a tour group will no doubt come following shortly thereafter.

Wise travelers try to avoid travel during Japan's three prime holiday seasons: New Year's (December 25th to January 10th), Golden Week (April 28th to May 6th), and O-bon (roughly July 21st to August 30th). Stay put during those weeks, and better yet, don't come to Japan until after the holidays. (On the other hand, downtown Tokyo can be pleasant then, as it's nearly empty.)

BY RAIL OR WATER

RAIL TRAVEL TIMES
Tokyo to:
Akita, 4 hrs.
Hiroshima, 4 hrs.
Kyoto, 2.5 hrs.
Nagano, 1 hr.
Sapporo, 10.5 hrs.
Osaka, 3 hrs.

FERRY TRAVEL TIMES
Osaka–Kagoshima, 15 hrs.
Kobe-Kyushu, 12 hrs.

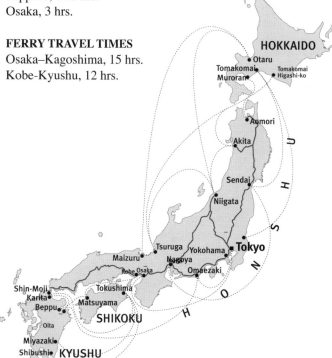

Travel opportunities by rail and ferry are too numerous to indicate on this basic map. However, the dotted lines indicate *shinkansen* routes; the solid lines indicate main ferry routes.

If surprises are unwanted and particularly if traveling on a budget, make use of an accommodation reservation service. In Tokyo, Kyoto, and Osaka, visit the Travel Information Centers (TIC). A TIC office is also available at Narita Airport, Terminal 2, 1st floor. They have listings of accommodations throughout Japan that are not only economical, but also accept foreigners. And they speak English. American Express offices and international-class hotel concierges can be helpful, too, even for nonmembers and nonguests.

Where is the tourist information office?	Kankō annaijo wa doko desu ka?	観光案内所はどこですか。
I'd like a sightseeing brochure/guide for here.	Kono machi no kankō pan-furetto o hoshii n'desu ga.	この町の観光パンフレットをほしいんですが。
Is there a ~ map?	~ chizu wa arimasu ka?	～地図はありますか。
road	dōro	道路
city	shinai	市内
Can I reserve a hotel room here?	Koko de hoteru no yoyaku ga dekimasu ka?	ここでホテルの予約ができますか。
I'd like to reserve a room in the city.	Shinai no hoteru o yoyaku shite kudasai.	市内のホテルを予約して下さい。
Is there a bus to the city?	Shinai e yuku basu wa arimasu ka?	市内へ行くバスはありますか。
Where can I catch the taxi/bus?	Takushii/Basu noriba wa doko desu ka?	タクシー／バス乗り場はどこですか。
Can I reserve a ~ at this office?	Koko de ~ no yoyaku ga dekimasu ka?	ここで～の予約ができますか。
I'd like to reserve a ~ in the city.	Shinai no ~ o yoyaku shite kudasai.	市内の～を予約して下さい。
western-style hotel	hoteru	ホテル
business hotel	bijinesu hoteru	ビジネスホテル
ryokan	ryokan	旅館
minshuku	minshuku	民宿
rental car	rentakā	レンタカー
How much is the taxi fare (to ~)?	(~ made) Takushii de ikura kurai desu ka?	(～まで) タクシーでいくらくらいですか。
Can I get there by bus?	Soko made basu wa arimasu ka?	そこまでバスはありますか。
Can I get there by train?	Soko made densha wa arimasu ka?	そこまで電車はありますか。

Can I get there by subway?	Soko made chikatetsu wa arimasu ka?	そこまで地下鉄はありますか。
Are there sightseeing buses?	Kankō basu wa arimasu ka?	観光バスはありますか。
Where can I buy a ticket?	Kippu wa doko de kau n'desu ka?	切符はどこで買うんですか。
Is there a/an ~ tour?	~ no kōsu wa arimasu ka?	～のコースはありますか。
half-day	hannichi	半日
all-day	ichi nichi	一日
morning	gozen	午前
afternoon	gogo	午後
Are meals included?	Shokujitsuki desu ka?	食事付きですか。
What time does it start?	Nan ji hatsu desu ka?	何時発ですか。
Where does it start?	Doko kara demasu ka?	どこから出ますか。

WAYS TO GO

Most travelers choose transportation by cost, comfort, and utility. Although comfortable, a taxi is outrageously expensive, and—in contrast to its meter—is the slowest thing around a major city during rush hour. Nonetheless, a person with luggage and in a cranky mood may opt to take a taxi. It's certainly great for sightseeing. Nonetheless, trains and subways are unquestionably the fastest and cheapest way to go in cities.

I want to go by ~.	~ de ikitai n'desu ga.	～で行きたいんですが。
taxi	takushii	タクシー
bus	basu	バス
car	kuruma	車
rental car	rentakā	レンタカー
subway	chikatetsu	地下鉄
train	densha	電車
express train	kyūkō	急行
bullet train	shinkansen	新幹線
plane	hikōki	飛行機
ship	fune	船
sightseeing boat	yūransen	遊覧船
sightseeing bus	kankō basu	観光バス
I want to walk.	Aruite ikitai n'desu ga.	歩いて行きたいんですが。

TAXI

Like their counterparts anywhere else, Japanese taxi drivers can be gracious chatterboxes or rude grumps. In Japan, their vehicles are always clean—white-glove clean. When entering and exiting, there's no need to touch the door. The driver will open and close it for you with a nifty remote lever from the driver's seat.

An empty taxi has a red indicator on the passenger-side dashboard, sometimes a mechanical flag but usually electrically lit. If a free taxi ignores you at night, it's likely because the driver is prowling for the perfect fare: an inebriated businessman who's missed the train and is heading back to the suburbs. Try the nearest deluxe hotel, where taxis are always waiting.

Feel free to practice your Japanese on the driver; some drivers like to chat with foreigners. But just in case, have your destination written in Japanese. Travel should be fun, not a blunder. Tips are not expected, but if change on the fare is less than ¥50, the driver will appreciate the left-overs. Hand him the fare, hesitate as he makes change, then knowingly say *Ee, ii desu*, "It's okay," and he'll keep the change.

Where is the taxi stand?	Takushii noriba wa doko desu ka?	タクシー乗り場はどこですか。
Where can I get a taxi?	Doko de takushii ni noremasu ka?	どこでタクシーに乗れますか。
Please call me a taxi.	Takushii o yonde kudasai.	タクシーを呼んで下さい。

What's the fare to ~?	~ made ikura desu ka?	～までいくらですか。
To the airport, please.	Kūkō e itte kudasai.	空港へ行って下さい。
I want to go to ~.	~ e ikitai n'desu ga.	～へ行きたいんですが。
Please go to ~.	~ made itte kudasai.	～まで行って下さい。
Please go to this address.	Kono jūsho e itte kudasai.	この住所へ行って下さい。
Please give me a brief tour of the city.	Machi no naka o hitotōri mawatte kudasai.	町の中をひととおりまわって下さい。

TAXI	AVAILABLE	NOT IN SERVICE	DISTANCE	DESTINATION
タクシー	空車	回送	距離	行き先
takushii	kūsha	kaisō	kyori	yukisaki

Go straight ahead.	Massugu itte kudasai.	まっすぐ行って下さい。
Turn ~ at the next corner, please.	Tsugi no kado o ~ e magatte kudasai.	次の角を〜へ曲がって下さい。
left	hidari	左
right	migi	右
Please turn left/right just up ahead.	Sugu hidari/migi e magatte kudasai.	すぐ左／右へ曲がって下さい。
Please hurry.	Isoide kudasai.	急いで下さい。
There's no hurry.	Isoganakute mo ii desu.	急がなくてもいいです。
Could you drive slower?	Mō sukoshi yukkuri unten shite kudasai.	もう少しゆっくり運転して下さい。
I'll get out at the intersection.	Sono kōsaten de orimasu.	その交差点でおります。
I'll get out at the next signal.	Tsugi no shingō de orimasu.	次の信号でおります。
Please stop over there.	Asoko de tomete kudasai.	あそこで止めて下さい。
Please stop here.	Koko de tomete kudasai.	ここで止めて下さい。
Please let me off here.	Koko de oroshite kudasai.	ここで下ろして下さい。
This place is fine.	Kono hen de ii desu.	この辺でいいです。
Stop here for a minute, please.	Koko de chotto tomete kudasai.	ここでちょっと止めて下さい。
Wait a moment, please.	Chotto matte ite kudasai.	ちょっと待っていて下さい。
How much is it?	Ikura desu ka?	いくらですか。
Keep the change.	Tsurisen wa totte oite kudasai.	つり銭はとっておいて下さい。

Where do you want go?
どこへ行きたいんですが。

Sorry, I can't seem to find It.
すみませんが見つからないようです。

Sorry, but I don't understand.
すみませんが分かりません。

I have to ask for directions.
道を聞かなくてはなりません。

Sorry, but I can't take you there now.
すみませんが今そこへは行けません。

I can/can't wait.
待つ事はできます／できません。

BUS

Buses usually have two doors, one in front and the other in the rear. One's the entrance and the other, the exit. Just follow the crowd to the appropriate door.

Bus fare is sometimes paid on boarding, sometimes on exiting. Figuring out the fare can be confusing, as fares are sometimes based on distance, however short the trip. Near the entrance door may be a ticket dispenser. Take a ticket. When you get off, give it to the driver, pretend to be stupid and hold out a handful of loose change. The driver will pick out the correct fare. (Then say thank you.)

Where is the bus stop?	Basutei wa doko desu ka?	バス停はどこですか。
Where can I get a bus to ~?	~ yuki no basutei wa doko desu ka?	～行きのバス停はどこですか。
What bus do I take for ~?	~ yuki no basu wa dore desu ka?	～行きのバスはどれですか。
When is the next bus to ~?	~ yuki no tsugi no basu wa itsu desu ka?	～行きの次のバスはいつですか。

Does this bus go to the ~ hotel?	Kono basu wa ~ hoteru ni tomarimasu ka?	このバスは～ホテルに止まりますか。
Does this bus go to ~?	Kono basu wa ~ made ikimasu ka?	このバスは～まで行きますか。
Is this the right bus to ~?	Kono basu wa ~ yuki desu ka?	このバスは～行きですか。
How far is it to ~?	~ made dono kurai arimasu ka?	～までどのくらいありますか。
How much is the fare?	Unchin wa ikura desu ka?	運賃はいくらですか。
How much is the fare to ~?	~ made ikura desu ka?	～までいくらですか。
Do I have to change buses?	Basu o norikaenakereba ikemasen ka?	バスを乗り換えなければいけませんか。
Where should I get off?	Doko de orireba ii desu ka?	どこでおりればいいですか。
Please tell me when to get off.	Itsu oritara ii ka oshiete kudasai.	いつおりたらいいか教えて下さい。
Can I get off at ~?	~ de oroshite moraemasu ka?	～でおろしてもらえますか。
I'll get off at ~.	~ de orimasu.	～でおります。
Let me off here, please.	Koko de oroshite kudasai.	ここでおろして下さい。
I'll get out at the next stop.	Tsugi de orimasu.	次でおります。
I'll get out at the second stop.	Tsugi no tsugi de orimasu.	次の次でおります。
I'll get out at the last stop.	Shuten de orimasu.	終点でおります。

FERRY

An island country, Japan lends itself to water travel, and ferries connect major ports from Hokkaido to Okinawa. Ferries aren't cheap, and they're not especially elegant by European standards. But they can be different. On longer, especially overnight, trips there are usually two choices for berthing: a semi-private cabin, or else the second-class deck, with open, shared areas for sitting, sleeping, and eating. Although cheaper, second-class can be noisy until the wee hours, and there is absolutely no privacy. As a foreigner and thus a curiosity, be prepared for stares, and too, invitations for beer, sake, and a little English and Japanese language practice.

Where do I board the ship to ~?	~ yuki no fune no noriba wa doko desu ka?	～行きの船の乗り場はどこですか。
What time does it board?	Jōsen jikan wa nan ji desu ka?	乗船時間は何時ですか。
What time does it depart?	Itsu shukkō shimasu ka?	いつ出航しますか。
Where is ~?	~ wa doko desu ka?	～はどこですか。
my berth	watashi no shindai	私の寝台
my cabin	watashi no senshitsu	私の船室
the toilet	toire	トイレ
the infirmary	imushitsu	医務室
the lifeboat	kyūmei bōto	救命ボート
a life jacket	kyūmei dōi	救命胴衣
the pier	sanbashi	桟橋
the port/harbor	minato	港
I'm quite seasick.	Funayoi ga hidoi desu.	船酔いがひどいです。
Can you get a doctor?	Isha o yonde moraemasu ka?	医者を呼んでもらえますか。

SHIP, BOAT 船 fune	FERRY フェリー ferii	PORT OF CALL 寄港地 kikōchi	STEAMSHIP COMPANY 汽船会社 kisen gaisha	PURSER パーサー pāsā
PASSENGER SHIP 客船 kyakusen	PIER 桟橋 sanbashi	PORT/ HARBOR 港 minato	CAPTAIN 船長 senchō	STEWARD スチュワード suchuwādo

BY AIR

飛

行

hikō
flight

For the most part, there are no surprises at the airport for the traveler. Indeed, airports are one of the few universal irritants for travelers everywhere. The process is predictable: check in, find the gate, board, wait out the flight, land (and perhaps clear customs and immigration), and retrieve your baggage.

At Japanese airports, someone usually has basic English skills, both at the terminal and on the plane, even for domestic flights.

Getting to and from the two largest international airports, Osaka and Tokyo, can take as long as a domestic flight itself. Allow plenty of time—no, lots of time—for getting to the airport. A bus (or taxi) from central/Tokyo to Narita can take up to 3 hours when traffic is heavy. Taking the train is generally much faster (about an hour) and more reliable.

If making a domestic connection from an international flight, remember that in both Osaka and Tokyo, there's a long ground connection involved. From Narita, Tokyo's international airport, to Haneda, its domestic airport, it takes two to three hours via ground travel (taxi, bus, or train).

As with train travel, air travel in Japan is not cheap.

AIRPORT CHECK-IN

Check-in presents few problems, other than navigating through group tours mustering for departure. If taking lots of baggage, know that on both domestic and international flights, counter personnel will be diligent about collecting excess baggage charges. Check your airline's website in advance for specific baggage size and weight restrictions.

I want to check in.	Chekku in shitai n'desu ga.	チェックインしたいんですが。
I want to make a reservation.	Hikōki no yoyaku o shitai n'desu ga.	飛行機の予約をしたいんですが。
I've made a reservation.	Yoyaku shimashita.	予約しました。
The reservation was confirmed in ~.	Yoyaku wa ~ de kakunin shite arimasu.	予約は〜で確認してあります。
I'd like to reconfirm my reservation.	Yoyaku no saikakunin o shitai n'desu ga.	予約の再確認をしたいんですが。
I want to change my flight.	Furaito o henkō shitai n'desu ga.	フライトを変更したいんですが。
I'd like to ~ my reservation.	Yoyaku o ~ shitai n'desu ga.	予約を〜したいんですが。
confirm	kakunin	確認
cancel	kyanseru	キャンセル
change	henkō	変更
Cancel this reservation, please.	Kono yoyaku o kyanseru shite kudasai.	この予約をキャンセルして下さい。

When is the next available flight to ~?	Tsugi ni noreru ~ yuki no bin wa nan ji desu ka?	次に乗れる〜行きの便は何時ですか。
Do you have any seats?	Seki wa arimasu ka?	席はありますか。
Is there a/an ~ flight?	~ no bin ga arimasu ka?	〜の便がありますか。
morning	gozen	午前
afternoon	gogo	午後
evening	yoru	夜
Is there an earlier flight?	Sore yori hayai bin ga arimasu ka?	それより早い便がありますか。

CHECK-IN チェックイン chekku in	DESTINATION 目的地 mokutekichi	DEPARTURE 出発 shuppatsu	ARRIVAL 到着 tōchaku	TIMETABLE 時刻表 jikokuhyō

GETTING AROUND

How much is it?	Ikura desu ka?	いくらですか。
How much is a one-way ticket to ~?	~ made katamichi ikura desu ka?	～まで片道いくらですか。
How much is a round trip ticket to ~?	~ made ōfuku ikura desu ka?	～まで往復いくらですか。
One ticket to ~, please.	~ yuki no kippu o ichi-mai kudasai.	～行きの切符を一枚下さい。
Round trip to ~, please.	~ made ōfuku ichi-mai kudasai.	～まで往復一枚下さい。
One-way to ~, please.	~ made katamichi ichi-mai kudasai.	～まで片道一枚下さい。
Window seat, please.	Madogawa no seki ni shite kudasai.	窓側の席にして下さい。
Aisle seat, please.	Tsūrogawa no seki ni shite kudasai.	通路側の席にして下さい。
No smoking seat, please.	Kin'enseki ni shite kudasai.	禁煙席にして下さい。
This is my baggage.	Kore ga watashi no nimotsu desu.	これが私の荷物です。
hand luggage	te nimotsu	手荷物
I'd like to check this.	Kore o azuketai n'desu ga.	これを預けたいんですが。
This one is fragile.	Waremono ga haitte imasu.	われ物が入っています。
How much is the excess baggage charge?	Chōka ryōkin wa ikura desu ka?	超過料金はいくらですか。
When is boarding time?	Tōjō kaishi wa nan ji desu ka?	搭乗開始は何時ですか。
Will this flight leave on time?	Kono bin wa yotei dōri demasu ka?	この便は予定通り出ますか。
How long is the delay?	Dono kurai okuremasu ka?	どのくらい遅れますか。

AIRPORT 空港 kūkō	**DOMESTIC FLIGHT** 国内線 kokunaisen	**AIRLINE TICKET** 航空券 kōkūken	**OPEN SEATING** 自由席 jiyūseki
AIRLINE COMPANY 航空会社 kōkū gaisha	**FLIGHT NUMBER** 便名 binmei	**ECONOMY CLASS** エコノミークラス ekonomii kurasu	**EXCESS BAG CHARGE** 超過料金 chōka ryōkin
AIRPLANE 飛行機 hikōki	**FARE** 運賃 unchin	**FIRST CLASS** ファーストクラス fāsuto kurasu	**BAGGAGE** 手荷物 te nimotsu
INTERNATIONAL FLIGHT 国際線 kokusaisen	**GATE** ゲート gēto	**NO SMOKING** 禁煙 kin'en	**SUITCASE** スーツケース sutsukēsu

ON THE AIRPLANE

Where is this seat?	Kono seki wa dono hen desu ka?	この席はどの辺ですか。
May I sit here?	Kono seki ni suwatte ii desu ka?	この席に座っていいですか。
May I get through?	Chotto tōshite kudasai.	ちょと通して下さい。

OCCUPIED	VACANT	SEAT NUMBER	BOARDING PASS	DRINK
使用中	空き	座席番号	搭乗券	飲み物
shiyōchū	aki	zaseki bangō	tōjōken	nomimono

BAGGAGE CLAIM

Where can I get my baggage?	Te nimotsu wa doko de uketori-masu ka?	手荷物はどこで受け取りますか。
I can't find my baggage.	Nimotsu ga mitsukarimasen.	荷物が見つかりません。
My luggage didn't come.	Nimotsu ga dete kimasen deshita.	荷物が出てきませんでした。
My luggage is lost.	Nimotsu ga nakunarimashita.	荷物がなくなりました。
My luggage is damaged.	Nimotsu ga kowarete imasu.	荷物がこわれています。

Do you have your claim tag?
手荷物引換証はありますか。

We'll deliver it to where you re staying.
お泊まり先へ届けます。

Do you have your ticket?
航空券はありますか。

Where shall we deliver it?
どちらへお届けでしょうか。

We will search for it.
お調べします。

We cannot locate it.
見つかりません。

It will come on the next flight.
次の便で来ます。

We will replace your luggage/contents.
荷物／中身を弁償します。

BAGGAGE CLAIM	CLAIM TAG/ TICKET	DAMAGED	LOST
荷物引取り	手荷物引換証	こわれている	なくした
nimotsu hikitori	te nimotsu hikikaeshō	kowatete iru	nakushita

IMMIGRATION

After you collect your luggage, you will pass through immigration and then customs. There is a separate immigration area for foreigners. An immigration agent will check your passport and the immigration card you filled out on the plane. You will also be fingerprinted.

If you arriving from certain Asian countries—the Philippines and Thailand come to mind—most likely the customs agent will give you more than a wave to the door. The customs people usually ask questions in basic English, but they may also show you pictures of what they are talking about: drugs and guns. Don't even joke about them. Handguns and drugs are illegal, and punishments are severe.

At customs, try not to line up behind a group of Japanese businessmen returning from a holiday. They're candidates for having their luggage meticulously searched for cigarettes, liquor, and pornography.

I'll stay at ~ hotel.	~ hoteru de tomarimasu.	〜ホテルに泊まります。
These are all my personal belongings.	Zenbu mi no mawarihin desu.	全部身のまわり品です。
This is a gift for a friend.	Kore wa yūjin e no miyagehin desu.	これは友人へのみやげ品です。

PASSPORT CONTROL 旅券検査 ryoken kensa	**RESIDENT (of Japan)** 居住者 kyojūsha	**NATIONALITY** 国籍 kokuseki	**SINGLE** 独身 dokushin
CUSTOMS 税関 zeikan	**NONRESIDENT** 非居住者 hikyojūsha	**ADDRESS IN JAPAN** 国内連絡先 kokunai renrakusaki	**OCCUPATION** 職業 shokugyō
PASSPORT パスポート pasupōto	**NAME** 名前 namae	**PERMANENT ADDRESS** 本籍 honseki	**PURPOSE OF VISIT** 旅行目的 ryokō mokuteki
VISA 査証 sashō	**FIRST NAME** 名前 namae	**DATE OF BIRTH** 生年月日 seinengappi	**PORT OF DEPARTURE** 出発地 shuppatsuchi
FOREIGNER 外国人 gaikokujin	**SURNAME** 姓 sei	**MARRIED** 既婚 kikon	**LENGTH OF STAY** 滞在期間 taizai kikan

Getting Around
BY RAIL

鉄
道

Except during Tokyo's rush-hour madness, trains, or *densha*, in Japan are delightful and obsessively punctual. Japan is a nation where train travel undertaken even for its own sake is a highly-regarded popular pastime.

Options on JR—Japan Rail—and its 20,000 kilometers of track and 25,000 daily runs are many. Trains come in diverse configurations, from rustic simplicity to glossy sleepers intended for honeymoon flirtations. There are local, rapid, express, and limited express trains. Falling under this last category is the so-called "bullet train," or *shinkansen*, running at silky-smooth high speeds, and charging fares to match its velocity.

testsudō
railway

The *shinkansen* and other express trains have first-class coaches called "green cars" (*guriin sha*) and lots of leg room. Rapid and local trains are generally no-frills commuter trains. Major cities have subway lines, usually connecting with JR and other railroads at major transfer, or *norikae*, stations. For intercity travel, trains running between city centers are extraordinarily convenient, as well as punctual.

Ticket prices are based on distance. There is a basic fare, with surcharges for express trains, reserved seats, green car seats, and sleepers. Between Tokyo and Kyoto, travel times for plane and train are about the same, as are fares. Japanese normally travel light on trains. Hauling luggage through stations is a nightmare, and trains have little storage space for more than carry-on luggage.

BUYING TICKETS

Train tickets are purchased at ticket machines for local, or basic, fares, with coins, bills, or prepaid cards ("Orange Cards"), or at ticket counters for longer routes and express/first-class surcharges. JR ticket counters and travel agencies generally accept credit cards. Subway tickets are purchased at ticket machines near the gates.

If pressed for time or simply perplexed about figuring out the fare, buy the cheapest ticket, get aboard, and pay the difference later at the destination station, either to the ticket-taker, at a fare adjustment window, or at an automatic fare adjustment machine. On non-commuter (e.g., long-distance) JR trains, adjustments and special surcharges can be paid directly to the conductor, who can also upgrade your ticket to the green car (for a surcharge), should you so desire.

PEAK TRAVEL DAYS: December 24 to January 10; March 21 to April 5; April 28 to May 6; July 21 to August 31.

SHINKANSEN TICKET

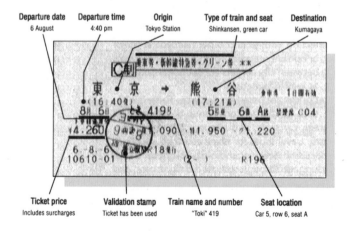

Departure date	Departure time	Origin	Type of train and seat	Destination
6 August	4:40 pm	Tokyo Station	Shinkansen, green car	Kumagaya

Ticket price	Validation stamp	Train name and number	Seat location
Includes surcharges	Ticket has been used	"Toki" 419	Car 5, row 6, seat A

TICKETS ON THE TRAIN

Except on local trains, a conductor will usually come through the train to check tickets and seat assignments. If you bought the cheapest ticket at the station to avoid calculating the fare, now is the time to pay the fare adjustment. The ticket shows where you're coming from, so just say (your destination) *desu*. The conductor will calculate the fare and issue a receipt. (Keep this receipt, as you'll need to present it together with the original ticket when exiting.) Likewise, if after boarding you've decided that you like the first-class seats better, take an empty seat in the green car and wait for the conductor to pass through. You'll usually be allowed to up-grade. Green car seats are often open seating, except on busy express trains to the suburbs.

Most express trains have separate cars for reserved and open/non-reserved seats. If you've chosen a seat at random, confirm that it's in the non-reserved car.

OPEN SEAT TICKET	ONE-WAY TICKET	BASIC FARE TICKET	PLATFORM TICKET
自由席券	片道切符	乗車券	入場券
jiyūsekiken	katamichi kippu	jōshaken	nyūjōken

RESERVED SEAT TICKET	ROUND-TRIP TICKET	EXPRESS TICKET	FARE ADJUSTMENT
指定席券	往復切符	急行券	清算
shiteisekiken	ōfuku kippu	kyūkōken	seisan

TICKET MACHINES

How do I get to ~?	~ e wa dō ittara ii desu ka?	~へはどういったらいいですか。
I can't read the fare information in Japanese.	Nihongo no ryōkin annai ga yomemasen.	日本語の料金案内が読めません。
How much is it to ~?	~ made ikura desu ka?	~までいくらですか。
No tickets came out when I put money in.	O-kane o ireta n'desu ga kippu ga demasen.	お金を入れたんですが切符がでません。
What does this mean?	Kore wa dō iu imi desu ka?	これはどういう意味ですか。
Please write it here.	Koko ni kaite kudasai.	ここに書いて下さい。
Please write ~ in kanji.	~ o kanji de kaite kudasai.	~を漢字で書いて下さい。
Please write ~ in romaji.	~ o rōmaji de kaite kudasai.	~をローマ字で書いて下さい。

TIME SCHEDULES

To use a train schedule—published monthly and found at bookstores and stations—learn to recognize the kanji of the stations you want. Not all schedules and route maps use romaji, or Roman lettering, and memorizing the Japanese characters will make station navigation easier, too.

TIMETABLE 時刻表 jikokuhyō	DESTINATION 行き先 yukisaki	AWAY FROM TOKYO 下り kudari	RAPID TRAIN 快速 kaisoku
ARRIVALS 到着 tōchaku	BOUND FOR ~ ~行き ~yuki	TRANSFER 乗り換え norikae	LOCAL EXPRESS 準急 junkyū
ARRIVAL TIME 到着時刻 tōchaku jikoku	IN DIRECTION OF ~ ~方面 ~ hōmen	TERMINATES AT ~ ~止まり ~ domari	EXPRESS TRAIN 急行 kyūkō
DEPARTURES 発車 hassha	VIA ~ ~経由 ~ keiyu	LOCAL TRAIN 各駅停車 kakueki teisha	LIMITED EXPRESS 特急 tokkyu
DEPARTURE TIME 発車時刻 hassha jikoku	TOWARDS TOKYO 上り nobori	LOCAL TRAIN 普通 futsū	BULLET TRAIN 新幹線 shinkansen

JAPAN RAIL PASS

If a journey by rail tickles the feet, consider a one-, two-, or three-week rail pass. To make it worth the value, however, one must travel long distances and/or often. A Japan Rail Pass entitles one to unlimited travel on all JR trains, including the *shinkansen*. Passes are available for ordinary and first-class seats, with surcharges for sleeping berths and private compartments. Note, however, that a JR pass won't get you onto a train belonging to one of the myriad private railroads.

You must plan ahead: the pass must be paid for prior to arrival in Japan. The selling agent will issue a voucher, which you can exchange for a pass at JR centers in most major JR train stations.

READING TIME SCHEDULES

Distance in kilometers Names of trains Train numbers Train origin and destination

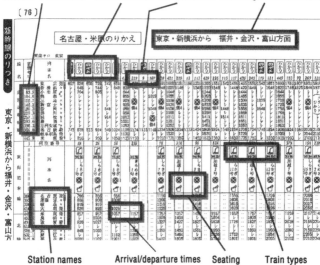

Station names Arrival/departure times Seating Train types

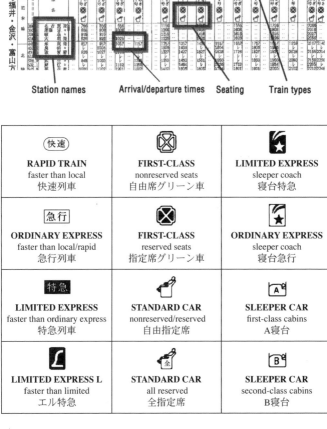

(快速) **RAPID TRAIN** faster than local 快速列車	⊠ **FIRST-CLASS** nonreserved seats 自由席グリーン車	★ **LIMITED EXPRESS** sleeper coach 寝台特急
急行 **ORDINARY EXPRESS** faster than local/rapid 急行列車	⊠ **FIRST-CLASS** reserved seats 指定席グリーン車	★ **ORDINARY EXPRESS** sleeper coach 寝台急行
特急 **LIMITED EXPRESS** faster than ordinary express 特急列車	⚷ **STANDARD CAR** nonreserved/reserved 自由指定席	A **SLEEPER CAR** first-class cabins A寝台
L **LIMITED EXPRESS L** faster than limited エル特急	⚷全 **STANDARD CAR** all reserved 全指定席	B **SLEEPER CAR** second-class cabins B寝台

GETTING AROUND

TICKET WINDOW

Can someone here speak English?	Eigo o hanaseru hito wa imasu ka?	英語を話せる人はいますか。
I'd like to go to ~.	~ ni ikitai n'desu ga.	~に行きたいんですが。
How do I get to ~?	~ e wa dō ittara ii desu ka?	~へはどう行ったらいいですか。
How much is it to ~?	~ made ikura desu ka?	~までいくらですか。
How much from here to ~?	Koko kara ~ made ikura desu ka?	ここから~までいくらですか。

What time is the next train?	Tsugi no densha wa nan ji desu ka?	次の電車は何時ですか。
Is there a train leaving around ~?	~ ji goro no densha wa arimasu ka?	~時ごろの電車はありますか。
What times does the train for ~ leave?	~ yuki no densha wa nan ji ni demasu ka?	~行きの電車は何時に出ますか。
When is the ~ to ~~?	~~ yuki no ~ wa nan ji desu ka?	~~行きの~は何時ですか。
next train	tsugi no densha	次の電車
first train	shihatsu densha	始発電車
last train	shūden	終電
How about the next train?	Tsugi no densha wa dō desu ka?	次の電車はどうですか。
How about a later time?	Motto osoi jikan wa dō desu ka?	もっと遅い時間はどうですか。
How about an earlier time?	Motto hayai jikan wa dō desu ka?	もっと早い時間はどうですか。
Any time is fine with me.	Nan ji de mo kamaimasen.	何時でもかまいません。

How long does the trip take?	Dono kurai jikan ga kakarimasu ka?	どのくらい時間がかかりますか。
Do I have to change trains?	Norikae ga arimasu ka?	乗り換えがありますか。
Where do I change trains?	Doko de norikae desu ka?	どこで乗り換えですか。
Can I stop along the way?	Tochū de noriori dekimasu ka?	途中で乗り降り出来ますか。
Is there an express?	Kyūkō wa arimasu ka?	急行はありますか。
Is there a sleeper?	Shindaisha wa tsuite imasu ka?	寝台車はついていますか。
From what track does it leave?	Nan ban sen kara demasu ka?	何番線から出ますか。

100

I'd like to reserve a seat on that train.	Sono densha no zaseki o yoyaku shitai n'desu ga.	その電車の座席を予約したいんですが。
I'd like to change this ticket to first-class.	Kono kippu o guriin sha ni kaetai n'desu ga.	この切符をグリーン車に変えたいんですが。
I'd like to ~ my reservation.	Yoyaku o ~ shiitai n'desu ga.	予約を~したいんですが。
confirm	kakunin	確認
cancel	kyanseru	キャンセル
change	henkō	変更
I'd like a refund, please.	Haraimodoshi o onegai shimasu.	払い戻しをお願いします。
A ticket to ~, please.	~ made kippu o ichi-mai kudasai.	~まで切符を一枚下さい。
one ticket	ichi-mai	一枚
two tickets	ni-mai	二枚
one way	katamichi	片道
round trip	ōfuku	往復
regular	futsūsha	普通車
first-class	guriin sha	グリーン車
open seating	jiyūseki	自由席
reserved seating	shiteiseki	指定席
window seat	madogawa no seki	窓側の席
alsle seat	tsūrogawa no seki	通路側の席
two adjacent seats	tsuzuite iru seki o futatsu	続いている席を二つ
in the front of the car	mae no hō no seki	前の方の席
in the back of the car	ushiro no hō no seki	後ろの方の席
nonsmoking seat	kin'enseki	禁煙席
smoking seat	kitsuenseki	喫煙席
seat with legroom	ichiban hiroi seki	一番広い席
seat as far as possible from smoking seats.	dekiru dake kitsuenseki kara hanarete iru seki	できるだけ喫煙席から離れている席。

That train is full.
この列車は満席です。

There are seats on the ~ train.
~に席がありますが。

How about the next train?
次の電車はどうですか。

Than are only ~ on that train.
この列車は~だけです。

Smoking or nonsmoking?
喫煙席、禁煙席のどちらにしますか。

There are no ~ on that train.
~はありません。

IN THE STATION

Interior station signs in major cities are usually marked in English, or at least in romaji. After a few trips through the system, you will probably recognize the different styles and color schemes of signs; what's on them, however, may remain a mystery. Some of the common markings on signs are shown on page 69. Remember that these kanji or kana characters won't be in isolation; other characters may be on either side of them. But if you can learn to recognize some of these groupings, you will find it much easier to get around major stations.

Where are the shinkansen tracks?	Shinkansen no hōmu wa doko desu ka?	新幹線のホームはどこですか。
Which train is it to ~?	~ yuki wa dore desu ka?	～行きはどれですか。
What track is the ~ line?	~ sen wa nan ban sen desu ka?	～線は何番線ですか。
Where is the ~ line?	~ sen wa doko desu ka?	～線はどこですか。
Is this the platform for the ~ line?	~ sen wa kono hōmu desu ka?	～線はこのホームですか。
Is this the right platform for the train to ~?	~ yuki no densha wa kono hōmu desu ka?	～行きの電車はこのホームですか。
What track does the train for ~ leave from?	~ yuki no densha wa nan ban sen kara demasu ka?	～行きの電車は何番線から出ますか。
Is this the train for ~?	Kono densha wa ~ yuki desu ka?	この電車は～行きですか。
Is this train a local/limited express?	Kono densha wa kakueki/tokkyū desu ka?	この電車は各駅／特急ですか。
Is this the subway to ~?	Kono chikatetsu wa ~ yuki desu ka?	この地下鉄は～行きですか。

It's a different train.
違う電車です。

It's on platform/track number ~.
～番線です。

It's on a different platform.
違うホームです。

It's already left.
もう出ました。

It's on the next platform.
となりのホームです。

NAVIGATING THE STATION

Mastering the large stations that serve as major transfer points is sometimes intimidating, especially because of long hikes between connections and endless stairways and escalators to everywhere. (Unless you're strong, better not to try to carry more than one large piece of luggage through such stations.) Shinjuku and Tokyo stations, for example, are especially confusing labyrinths, even to the initiated. But stations are usually well-marked, with important signs in English.

TRAINS: JR stations are generally above ground and entered from street level. Entrances/exits are usually identified by compass points, such as *higashi guchi*, or east entrance/exit. (At Tokyo Station, main exits are also identified as the Yaesu or Marunouchi sides.) Ticket machines and coin lockers are often near entrances. Local JR train lines, as well as subways, are identified by name and color. (Trains of the same line going in opposite directions do not always share the same platform; double-check the signs.)

Barring earthquakes and typhoons, JR trains (and virtually all other trains) are almost always punctual down to the minute, adhering to strict timetables, copies of which are mounted in poster form on platforms.

SUBWAYS: Despite the often convoluted nature of their layouts, navigating subway stations is easy, for they are extremely well-marked with signs and maps, and in English. In Tokyo, subway stations usually have a number of exits—marked A1, A2, etc.—leading up to several street-level places, including department store interiors. Well-marked maps showing exactly where exits surface are numerous.

AVOID THE CROWDS

Avoid intercity train travel during the holiday seasons, when *shinkansen* run at 100 to 200 percent capacity: literally standing room only. On the other hand, urban Tokyo during the holiday season becomes a delight, as it and its trains grow empty.

You should also avoid urban subways and commuter trains during *morning* and evening rush hours, unless being crushed like packed tomatoes is appealing. If a train looks beyond redemption, the next one may have more room. Also try the first and last car of a train.

ON THE TRAIN

Unless you're trapped amidst a bunch of restless school children, trains are generally a pleasure. On the long-distance expresses, seats are nice, sometimes exquisite. Local train seats, unfortunately, can be uncomfortable for tall people.

Eating on the train is perfectly acceptable, even encouraged by JR; some trains even have trays that fold out of the backs of seats, airplane-style. Food and drinks, including beer, can be purchased at stations and brought on board, or purchased on express trains and *shinkansen*. Best, however, is the *ekiben*, a usually delightful form of the bentō, the traditional Japanese box lunch. Most areas have unique *ekiben*, featuring local specialties. Get one on the train, or from a platform vendor before boarding. It's Japanese cuisine at its finest and funnest.

Where does this train go?	Kono densha wa doko yuki desu ka?	この電車はどこ行きですか。
Does this train stop at ~?	Kono densha wa ~ ni tomari-masu ka?	この電車は〜に止まりますか。
What is the next station?	Tsugi no eki wa doko desu ka?	次の駅はどこですか。
The next stop is ~, isn't it?	Tsugi wa ~ desu ne.	次は〜ですね。
Is ~ the next stop?	Tsugi wa ~ desu ka?	次は〜ですか。
Where are we passing through now?	Ima doko o hashitte imasu ka?	今どこを走っていますか。
What station is this?	Koko wa doko no eki desu ka?	ここはどこの駅ですか。
Please tell me when we reach ~.	~ ni tsuitara oshiete kudasai.	〜に着いたら教えて下さい。
When do we get to ~?	~ ni wa itsu tsukimasu ka?	〜にはいつ着きますか。
How long will we stop here?	Koko ni wa dono kurai tomarimasu ka?	ここにはどのくらい止まりますか。
What time should I be back on board?	Nan ji made ni densha ni modotte konakereba nari-masen ka?	何時までに電車にもどってこなければなりませんか。
Where do I transfer for ~?	~ e wa doko de norikaeru n'desu ka?	〜へはどこで乗り換えるんですか。
May I sit here?	Kono seki ni suwatte ii desu ka?	この席に座っていいですか。
I think this is my seat.	Koko wa watashi no seki da to omoimasu ga.	ここは私の席だと思いますが。
Can I smoke?	Tabako o sutte mo ii desu ka?	たばこを吸ってもいいですか。

EXITING THE STATION

Getting out of most stations is quite easy. If you need to pay a fare adjustment, there will be a marked window at the exit for that purpose, or sometimes an automatic fare adjustment machine. Otherwise, you can just hand the ticket to the taker at the gate, who will calculate the difference for you (and call after you if you've tried to slip through without paying).

Is there a place to store luggage for a few days?	Ni san nichi nimotsu o azukatte kureru tokoro wa arimasu ka?	2,3日荷物をあずかってくれるところはありますか。
baggage storage	te nimotsu ichi ji azukarijo	手荷物一時預かり所
I'd like to store my luggage.	Nimotsu o azuketai n'desu ga.	荷物をあずけたいんですが。
Which exit do I take for ~?	~ wa dono deguchi ga ii desu ka?	～はどの出口がいいですか。
Where is the nearest ~?	Ichiban chikai ~ wa doko desu ka?	一番近い～はどこですか。
How long does it take to go to the ~ by taxi?	~ made takushii de nan pun kurai desu ka?	～までタクシーで何分くらいですか。
hotel	hoteru	ホテル
business hotel	bijinesu hoteru	ビジネスホテル
ryokan	ryokan	旅館
minshuku	minshuku	民宿
Is it far from here?	Sore wa koko kara tōi desu ka?	それはここから遠いですか。

ESSENTIAL VERBS

to take a taxi タクシーに乗る takushii ni noru	to pay 払う harau	to change, modify 変更する henkō suru
to take a train 電車に乗る densha ni noru	to pay a fare adjustment 清算する seisan suru	cancel 取り消す torikesu
to take a bus バスに乗る basu ni noru	to plan, expect 予定する yotei suru	to lose something なくす nakusu

PROBLEMS AND REQUESTS

Problems on the train will be few: someone's sitting in your seat, you're sitting in someone else's seat, smokers are smoking where they shouldn't, losing a ticket, bratty children. If a polite request to a fellow passenger doesn't work or seems inappropriate, hunt down the conductor.

Be nice and courteous to the conductor, for he or she can smooth out problems. The conductor is boss of the train. They usually don't speak much English, but they're patient with foreigners' queries and problems. If in need of the conductor and you can't wait for one to pass by, check the green car, which usually has its own conductors in classy white suits and shoes.

Sorry, but I think this is a non-smoking area.	Sumimasen ga koko wa kin'enseki da to omoimasu ga.	すみませんがここは禁煙席だと思いますが。
Your children are disturbing me.	O-taku no o-ko-san ga chotto nigiyaka na n'desu ga.	おたくのお子さんがちょっとにぎやかなんですが。
Your children are kicking my seat.	O-taku no o-ko-san ga watashi no seki o kette iru n'desu ga.	おたくのお子さんが私の席をけっているんですが。
Can you be a little quieter?	Mō sukoshi shizuka ni shite kuremasen ka?	もう少し静かにしてくれませんか。
There's someone in my seat.	Watashi no seki ni dareka ga suwatte imasu.	私の席に誰かが座っています。
Someone's smoking in the non-smoking car.	Kin'ensha de tabako o sutte iru hito ga imasu.	禁煙車でたばこを吸っている人がいます。
I'm confused and lost.	Doko da ka sappari wakari-masen.	どこだかさっぱり分かりません。
I lost my ticket.	Kippu o nakushimashita.	切符をなくしました。
I left my ~ on the train.	Densha ni ~ o okiwasure-mashita.	電車に～を置き忘れました。
I lost my ~.	~ o nakushimashita.	～をなくしました。
luggage	nimotsu	荷物
wallet	saifu	財布
passport	pasupōto	パスポート
money	o-kane	お金
camera	kamera	カメラ
coat	kōto	コート
... and other things	to hoka no mono	とほかの物

What should I do?	Dō sureba ii deshō ka?	どうすればいいでしょうか。
Please write a theft report.	Tōnanshōmeisho o tsukutte kudasai.	盗難証明書を作って下さい。
Can you let me off at ~?	~ de oroshite moraemasu ka?	～でおろしてもらえますか。
Can I upgrade to first class?	Guriin sha e utsuremasu ka?	グリーン車へ移れますか。
Can I refund this ticket?	Kono kippu o haraimodose-masu ka?	この切符を払い戻せますか。
Can I change my seat?	Seki o utsutte mo ii desu ka?	席を移ってもいいですか。

What station did you come from?
どこの駅から乗りましたか。

What seat were you in?
どの席に座っていましたか。

What train were you on?
どの電車に乗っていましたか。

What size?
大きさはどれくらいですか。

I'll try to find someone who speaks English.
誰か英語を話せる人をさがしてみます。

What color?
何色ですか。

I'll contact the stations ahead to check for it
駅に連絡して調べてもらいましょう。

Please write down your name, telephone number, and address.
この紙に、氏名、電話番号、住所を書いて下さい。

Where are you sitting?
席はどこですか。

Yes, you can upgrade.
グリーン車へ移ることができます。

I'll try to take care of it.
私が何とかしましょう。

You can't upgrade now.
今はグリーン車へは移れません。

Where are you getting off?
どこでおりますか。

I'll let you know later if it's possible.
もし大丈夫なら後でお知らせします。

It can't be done right now.
今すぐにはできません。

There is an extra charge for first class.
余分にお金がかかります。

Getting Along

GETTING ALONG

Getting Along
EATING

Where to eat is problematic. The choices are considerable, copious, captivating. Talk a walk along main streets and back streets, too, before deciding.

Two big decisions: what to eat, and what to spend. There is, of course, traditional Japanese cuisine. Then, there are imports from other parts of Asia, and the West. In between are an infinite number of mutations and adaptations, some of which are local delicacies, while others are merely odd flights of fancy, like spaghetti in a hot dog bun.

shokuji
meals

Japanese spend ample money on food, drink, and ambiance. Long and expensive business meals are especially common, due to the view that business relationships involve constant and lavish nurturing. Aside from business, however, the tininess of urban Japanese homes also plays a role in the popularity of eating out. Few people want to spend an evening at home in a claustrophobic shoe box, and so there are many eateries with small places to sit, drink, and eat.

Even as a restaurant's appeal lies not only in its food, the appeal of the food itself extends beyond mere taste. The guest who appreciates the presentation and aesthetics of a meal will be rewarded with a grateful host. Maybe even grateful enough to offer seconds.

Final note: Most Japanese people consider it rude to walk and eat at the same time. In Japan, it's proper to sit down on something and then eat, even a simple snack.

FINDING SOMETHING TO EAT

Can you recommend a good restaurant nearby?	Kono chikaku no ii resutoran o oshiete kudasai.	この近くのいいレストランを教えて下さい。
Someplace not too expensive.	Amari takakunai mise ga ii desu.	あまり高くない店がいいです。
Someplace quiet.	Shizuka-na fun'iki no mise ga ii desu.	静かなふんいきの店がいいです。
Is there a/an ~ restaurant near here?	Kono chikaku ni ~ (ryōri) no mise wa arimasu ka?	この近くに～料理の店はありますか。
local cuisine	kyōdo	郷土
Japanese	Nihon	日本
French	Furansu	フランス
Italian	Itaria	イタリア
Indian	Indo	インド
Thai	Tai	タイ
Korean	Kankoku	韓国
Chinese	Chūka	中華
I'd like to try the best local food/cuisine.	Jimoto no meibutsu ryōri o tabetai n'desu ga.	地元の名物料理を食べたいんですか。
Can you recommend a place?	O-susume no mise wa arimasu ka?	おすすめの店はありますか。
Can you make reservations for me?	Koko de yoyaku o shite moraemasu ka?	ここで予約をしてもらえますか。

ESSENTIAL VERBS

to be hungry おなかがすく o-naka ga suku	**to eat** 食べる taberu	**to take (time)** かかる kakaru
to be thirsty のどがかわく nodo ga kawaku	**to eat out** 外食する gaishoku suru	**to make, prepare** 作る tsukuru
to drink 飲む nomu	**to order** 注文する chūmon suru	**to pay** 払う harau

FOOD, FAMILIAR AND NOT

Having decided where to eat, deciding what to eat is perhaps easier. Plastic facsimiles of menu offerings are usually outside near restaurant entrances, and menus frequently have color photographs. Not that they're guaranteed to be accurate. It's been known for a plastic slice of pizza to translate into a grilled ketchup-and-cheese sandwich.

On menus, traditional Japanese food is usually written with Chinese characters, but most other foods and drinks appear in kana, especially katakana. An ability to read katakana can be very helpful in deciphering menus; a sense of imagination is also a boon, as when translating *hamu eggu sando* into ham-and-egg sandwich.

Smoking is the norm in most restaurants, and even a nonsmoker in a cramped restaurant can expect clouds of smoke over his plate. "No smoking" tables are usually the least desirable ones.

One can eat rather cheaply in Japan, in stand-up, or *tachigui*, noodle shops and wedged-in-a-nook yakitori stands. Simple and lacking in elegance, but substantial and satisfying.

Stop by convenience stores like 7-Eleven or Lawsons; huge profits are made on carry-out foods, from bento box lunches to cheeseburgers. A number of traditional Japanese foods—*bentō*, *onigiri*, *o-den*, *rāmen*—can be bought for decent prices, and are made fresh daily.

Nearly every town and village has a local specialty. If traveling outside of Tokyo and Osaka, you might want to learn what the local delicacy is and try it for a change of pace.

Foreigners with a hankering for American-style fast-food and family restaurants will find comfort in Kentucky Fried Chicken and Denny's, along with Japanese imitations like Mos Burger (pronounced with an o as in open) and Royal Host. Western cuisine is a mixed plate in Japan. At the finest of Western-style restaurants—in luxury hotels, for example—food will look somehow too perfect, without personality or initiative. Tastes fine but looks like plastic. Some cuisines, like Italian, haven't translated too well in Japan: sauces lack spunk and taste, and often come with odd inclusions like corn kernels and octopus tentacles. On the other hand, Indian and Pakistani restaurants are numerous and usually managed by Indians and Pakistanis. They typically serve fine food in large portions.

PREPARATIONS

Is there a table for ~ people?	~ nin desu ga seki wa tore-masu ka?	～人ですが席は取れますか。
I have a reservation.	Yoyaku shite arimasu.	予約してあります。
Where is the restroom?	Toire wa doko desu ka?	トイレはどこですか。
May I use your rest-room?	Chotto toire o karitai n'desu ga.	ちょっとトイレを借りたいんですが。
I'd like to see a menu, please.	Menyū o misete kudasai.	メニューを見せて下さい。
Is there an Engllsh menu?	Eigo no menyū wa arimasu ka?	英語のメニューはありますか。
A little more time, please.	Mō sukoshi matte kudasai.	もう少し待って下さい。

We haven't any tables.
席はいっぱいです。

Are you ready to order?
ご注文はお決まりですか。

Just yourself?
お一人ですか。

Do you want something to drink?
お飲み物はいかがですか。

How many in your group?
何名様ですか。

I'll return when you're ready to order.
ご注文が決まったらまたうかがいます。

ORDER 注文 chūmon	MEAL 食事 shokuji	RESERVED 予約席 yoyakuseki	2nd SERVING お代わり o-kawari	NO SMOKING 禁煙 kin'en
FOOD 食べ物 tabemono	MENU メニュー menyū	WAITER / WAITRESS ウエーター／ウエートレス uētā/uētoresu	EATING OUT 外食 gaishoku	SHARE A TABLE 相席 aiseki
BREAKFAST 朝食 chōshoku 朝ご飯 asa gohan	LUNCH 昼食 chūshoku 昼ご飯 hiru gohan	DINNER 夕食 yūshoku 夕ご飯, 夕飯 yū gohan, yūhan	SET MENU WESTERN FOOD セット setto	SET MENU JAPANESE FOOD 定食 teishoku

DRINKS, HOT AND COLD

I'd like a drink first.	Mazu nanika nomitai n'desu ga.	まず何か飲みたいんですが。
Do you have ~?	~ ga arimasu ka?	～がありますか。
I'll have ~.	~ o kudasai.	～を下さい。
I don't want ~.	~ wa kekkō desu.	～はけっこうです。

DRINK 飲み物 nomimono	**DECAF COFFEE** カフェイン抜きのコーヒー kafeinnuki no kōhii	**LEMON TEA** レモンティー remon tii	**COCOA** ココア kokoa
COLD (drink, adj.) 冷たい tsumetai	**ICED COFFEE** アイスコーヒー aisu kōhii	**MILK TEA** ミルクティー miruku tii	**LEMONADE** レモネード remonēdo
HOT (drink, adj.) 熱い atsui	**TEA** お茶 o-cha	**COLA** コーラ kōra	**JUICE** ジュース jūsu
ICE 氷 kōri	**GREEN TEA** 緑茶 ryokucha	**MILK** ミルク miruku	**APPLE JUICE** リンゴジュース ringo jūsu
WATER 水 mizu	**OOLONG TEA** ウーロン茶 ūroncha	**SKIM MILK** スキムミルク sukimu miruku	**GRAPEFRUIT JUICE** グレープフルーツジュース gurēpufurūtsu jūsu
PLAIN HOT WATER 白湯 sayu	**BARLEY TEA** 麦茶 mugicha	**LOWFAT MILK** ローファトミルク rōfatto miruku	**ORANGE JUICE** オレンジジュース orenji jūsu
COFFEE コーヒー kōhii	**BLACK TEA** 紅茶 kōcha	**COLD MILK** 冷たいミルク tsumetai miruku	**PINEAPPLE JUICE** パイナップルジュース painappuru jūsu
AMERICAN COFFEE アメリカン（コーヒー） amerikan (kōhii)	**ICED TEA** アイスティー aisu tii	**HOT MILK** ホットミルク hotto miruku	**TOMATO JUICE** トマトジュース tomato jūsu

THE HARD STUFF

In a social gathering, one who shuns alcohol may be the group's oddball. Japanese men, in particular, find liberation in alcohol. Improper behavior under the influence is socially acceptable and excusable. Tell the boss he's a daft airhead, and the next morning all is forgiven, and hopefully forgotten. Even lewd behavior is usually excused because of drinking; male behavior towards women can become quite aggressive and suggestive.

Never fill your own glass—someone else will keep it full. Your responsibility is to keep other glasses filled. Doing so will help bring you into the group. Drinking supposedly strengthens relationships both in friendship and business, and there are countless establishments for evening drinks, from *sunakku bā*—much like Western lounges—to *nomi-ya*, more traditional Japanese drinking establishments.

I'd like ~.	~o kudasai.	～を下さい。
I'll have ~.	~ ni shimasu.	～にします。
I don't want ~.	~ wa kekkō desu.	～はけっこうです。
Do you have ~?	~ ga arimasu ka?	～がありますか。
Cheers!	Kanpai.	乾杯。

ALCOHOLIC DRINKS 酒 sake	BEER ビール biiru	WINE ワイン wain	SWEET 甘口の amakuchi no
JAPANESE SAKE 日本酒 nihonshu	WHISKY AND WATER 水割り mizuwari	RED 赤 aka	DRY 辛口の karakuchi no
RICE WINE 酒 sake	ON THE ROCKS オンザロック on za rokku	WHITE 白 shiro	PLUM WINE 梅酒 umeshu
SPECIAL RICE WINE 清酒 seishu	BRANDY ブランデー burandē	ROSÉ ロゼ roze	CHAMPAGNE シャンパン, シャンペン shanpan, shanpen

ORDERING

Do you have ~?	~ ga arimasuka?	〜がありますか。
I'll have ~.	~ o kudasai.	〜を下さい。
I don't want ~.	~ wa kekkō desu.	〜はけっこうです。
What's the house specialty?	Koko no o-susume ryōri wa nan desu ka?	ここのおすすめ料理は何ですか。
Is there a set menu?	Setto menyū wa arimasu ka?	セットメニューはありますか。
I'll take what you recommend.	Anata no o-susume ryōri ni shimasu.	あなたのおすすめ料理にします。
I'll have that.	Sore o moraimasu.	それをもらいます。
Give me the same as that.	Are to onaji mono o kudasai.	あれと同じものを下さい。
How long does it take?	Dono kurai kakarimasu ka?	どのくらいかかりますか。
How many minutes will it take?	Nan pun kurai de dekimasu ka?	何分くらいでできますか。
Can I have it right away?	Sugu dekimasu ka?	すぐできますか。
How do you eat this?	Tabekata o oshiete kudasai.	食べ方を教えて下さい。
May I have a little more, please?	Mō sukoshi itadakemasu ka?	もう少しいただけますか。
May I have some more, please?	Mō sukoshi kudasai.	もう少し下さい。
Do you have a breakfast special?	Mōningu sābisu wa arimasu ka?	モーニングサービスはありますか。
I'll have the breakfast special.	Mōningu sābisu o onegai shimasu.	モーニングサービスをお願いします。

If eating with Japanese companions (or even if not), say *itada-kimasu* just before starting the meal. When finished, saying *gochisōsama deshita* will be appreciated by your host. Say both with sincerity.

Itadakimasu.
いただきます。

Gochisōsama deshita.
ごちそうさまでした。

BREAKFAST

A traditional Japanese breakfast of rice, cold fish, miso soup, and raw egg rarely excites Western tastes. Easy to find, however, are Western-style breakfasts, with Japanese twists such as green salads garnished with corn. Most restaurants serving breakfast have decently-priced "morning sets" that may include toast, eggs, salad, and coffee.

CORN FLAKES コーンフレーク kōn furēku	**BACON AND EGGS** ベーコンエッグ bēkon eggu	**PANCAKES** ホットケーキ hotto kēki	**ROLL** ロールパン rōrupan
OATMEAL オートミール ōtomiiru	**SAUSAGE AND EGGS** ソーセージと卵 sōsēji to tamago	**JAM** ジャム jarnu	**TOAST** トースト tōsuto
HAM AND EGGS ハムエッグ hamu eggu	**CHEESE OMELET** チーズオムレツ chiizu omuretsu	**BREAD** パン pan	**SALAD** サラダ sarada

DAIRY PRODUCTS

DAIRY PRODUCTS 乳製品 nyūseihin	**MILK** 牛乳 gyūnyū	**BUTTER** バター batā	**CHEESE** チーズ chiizu
FRESH CREAM 生クリーム nama kuriimu	**MILK** ミルク miruku	**MARGARINE** マーガリン māgarin	**YOGURT** ヨーグルト yōguruto

EGGS

EGG 卵 tamago	**SOFT-BOILED EGG** 半熟卵 hanjukutamago	**FRIED EGG** 目玉焼き medamayaki	**OMELETTE** オムレツ omuretsu
BOILED EGG ゆで卵 yudetamago	**HARD-BOILED EGG** 固ゆで卵 katayudetamago	**SCRAMBLED EGGS** いり卵 iritamago	**RICE OMELETTE** オムライス omuraisu

117

FRUIT

FRUIT 果物 kudamono	GRAPEFRUIT グレープフルーツ gurēpufurūtsu	ORANGE オレンジ orenji	PINEAPPLE パイナップル painappuru
APPLE りんご ringo	GRAPES ぶどう budō	PAPAYA パパイア papaia	PLUM すもも sumomo
APRICOT あんず anzu	KIWI キウイフルーツ kiuifurūtsu	PEACH もも momo	RAISIN 干しぶどう hoshibudo
BANANA バナナ banana	LEMON レモン remon	PEAR 洋なし yōnashi	RASPBERRY 木いちご ki ichigo
CHERRY さくらんぼ sakuranbo	MANDARIN ORANGE みかん mikan	JAPANESE PEAR なし nashi	STRAWBERRY いちご ichigo
CHESTNUT くり kuri	MELON メロン meron	PERSIMMON かき kaki	WATERMELON すいか suika

VEGETABLES

VEGETABLE 野菜 yasai	BAMBOO SHOOTS 竹の子 takenoko	CARROT にんじん ninjin	CORN とうもろこし tōmorokoshi
ASPARAGUS アスパラガス asuparagasu	BEAN SPROUTS もやし moyashi	CAULIFLOWER カリフラワー karifurawā	CUCUMBER きゅうり kyūri
AVOCADO アボカド abokado	CABBAGE キャベツ kyabetsu	CELERY セロリ serori	EGGPLANT なす nasu

VEGETABLES (cont'd)

GREEN PEPPER	LOTUS ROOT	ONION	SPINACH
ピーマン	れんこん	たまねぎ	ほうれん草
piiman	renkon	tama negi	hōrensō
JAPANESE RADISH	**MUSHROOMS**	**PEAS**	**SQUASH**
だいこん	きのこ	えんどう豆	かぼちゃ
daikon	kinoko	endōmame	kabocha
LETTUCE	**JAPANESE MUSHROOM**	**POTATO**	**TOMATO**
レタス	しいたけ	じゃがいも	トマト
retasu	shiitake	jagaimo	tomato

SEAFOOD

FISH	EEL	PRAWN	SHRIMP
魚	うなぎ	車海老	甘海老
sakana	unagi	kuruma ebi	ama ebi
GRILLED FISH	**HALIBUT**	**RED SNAPPER**	**SHRIMP, PRAWN**
焼き魚	おひょう	鯛	海老
yakizakana	ohyō	tai	ebi
ABALONE	**LOBSTER**	**SALMON**	**SQUID, CUTTLEFISH**
あわび	伊勢海老	鮭	いか
awabi	ise ebi	sake	ika
BONITO	**MACKEREL**	**SCALLOP**	**TROUT**
かつお	さば	ほたて	ます
katsuo	saba	hotate	masu
CLAMS	**OCTOPUS**	**SEAWEED**	**TUNA**
はまぐり	たこ	わかめ	まぐろ
hamaguri	tako	wakame	maguro
CRAB	**OYSTER, CLAM**	**SHELLFISH**	**SEA URCHIN**
かに	牡蠣	貝	うに
kani	kaki	kai	uni

MEAT

MEAT 肉 niku	**STEAK** ステーキ sutēki	**LAMB** 子羊 kohitsuji	**TURKEY** 七面鳥 shichimenchō
BACON ベーコン bēkon	**GROUND BEEF** 牛のひき肉 gyū no hikiniku	**LIVER** レバー rebā	**SAUSAGE** ソーセージ sōsēji
BEEF 牛肉 gyūniku	**SALISBURY STEAK** ハンバーグ hanbāgu	**MUTTON** マトン maton	**CHICKEN** とり肉 tori niku
KOBE BEEF 和牛 wagyū	**HAM** ハム hamu	**PORK** 豚肉 buta niku	**WHALE** くじら kujira
WELL-DONE よく焼けた yoku yaketa	**BAKED** 天火で焼いた tenpi de yaita	**FRIED** 揚げた ageta	**SMOKED** くん製にした kunsei ni shita
MEDIUM 中ぐらいに chūgurai ni	**BARBECUED** 直火で焼いた jikabi de yaita	**GRILLED** 網焼きにした amiyaki ni shita	**STUFFED** 詰め物にした tsumemono ni shita
RARE 生焼けに namayake ni	**BOILED/STEWED** 煮込んだ nikonda	**SAUTEED** いためた itameta	**RAW** 生の nama no

WESTERN FARE

So-called Western food is nearly everywhere. In coffee shops and small cafes, the menu fare will usually include variations on the Western foods below. The flavor may be somewhat bland for Western tastes.

SOUP	SANDWICH	CURRIED RICE	CHEESECAKE
スープ	サンドイッチ	カレーライス	チーズケーキ
sūpu	sandoitchi	karē raisu	chiizukēki
SPAGHETTI	**HAMBURGER**	**DESSERT**	**PIE**
スパゲッティ	ハンバーガー	デザート	パイ
supagetti	hanbāgā	dezāto	pai
SALAD	**PIZZA**	**CAKE**	**ICE CREAM**
サラダ	ピザ	ケーキ	アイスクリーム
sarada	piza	kēki	aisu kuriimu

EXTRAS

Is there any ~?	~ wa arimasuka?	～はありますか。
Please bring me ~.	~ o motte kite kudasai.	～を持って来て下さい。

SEASONING	KETCHUP	PEPPER	SOY SAUCE
調味料	ケッチャップ	こしょう	しょう油
chōmiryō	kechappu	koshō	shōyu
GARLIC	**MAYONNAISE**	**RED PEPPER**	**SUGAR**
にんにく	マヨネーズ	唐辛子	砂糖
ninniku	mayonēzu	tōgarashi	satō
GINGER	**MUSTARD**	**SALT**	**VINEGAR**
しょうが	からし	塩	酢
shōga	karashi	shio	su
JAPANESE HORSERADISH	**OIL**	**SESAME SEED**	**WORCESTER-SHIRE SAUCE**
わさび	油、オイル	ごま	ソース
wasabi	abura, oiru	goma	sōsu

JAPANESE FOOD

If you're rich or have accepted an invitation from a Japanese person who highly values your relationship, you may find yourself eating at a *ryōtei*, a thoroughly Japanese restaurant that serves *kaiseki ryōri*, the finest in Japanese cuisine. Labor-intensive and located in some of the most elegant settings, *ryōtei* are very expensive.

The *izakaya* is an eminently affordable Japanese restaurant, usually a working-class establishment, and often identified by the red paper lanterns (*aka-chōchin*) hanging outside. Food is diverse, and drinks flow freely. *Izakaya* are casual and usually offer warm ambiance. Even more rustic are *yatai*, street carts set up as small shops—a few chairs, hanging lanterns, lights—and dishing up *rāmen* noodles or perhaps *o-den*, a boiled stew of mostly vegetarian foods. Some other typical types of Japanese cuisine are:

YAKITORI, the most standard *izakaya* fare. Yakitori is various chicken parts skewered on bamboo slivers and broiled over open charcoal. Usually, *izakaya* patrons will wash down their chicken with *nihonshu*, or Japanese sake, or cold beer.

NOODLES, including *rāmen* (Chinese style), *soba* (buckwheat), and *udon* (wheat). A wide diversity of places, from cheap to highbrow, offers diverse menus of *soba* and/or *udon*, usually including regional specialties. *Rāmen* shops usually offer only ramen.

SUSHI, an art in itself, and well-known even to non-natives. To watch a sushi chef serving up orders is a pleasure. There are cheap sushi shops, sometimes using circular conveyor belts from which the customer selects his own plates. Raw seafood—and other goodies, as well, such as cooked egg, or cucumber—and rice sculpted into near art.

SASHIMI, a simpler presentation of raw seafood than sushi, and less confusing to order. One asks for a particular fish or shellfish, and it's served sliced and garnished.

TEMPURA, which runs the gamut from delicate and featherlike to heavy like an oily sponge. At its best, tempura is expensive. Tempura restaurants typically offer three different courses in price and fanciness.

NABE, a hearty dish for when the snows start to fall and the air turns brittle. A variety of fresh vegetables and meat are put into a heavy pot with water, and cooked over an open flame right at the table.

JAPANESE FOOD

JAPANESE FOOD 和食 washoku	UNCOOKED RICE 米 kome	COOKED WHITE RICE ご飯 gohan	BOWL OF COOKED RICE どんぶり、茶碗 donburi, chawan
BEAN CURD 豆腐 tōfu	BEAN-JAM BUN まんじゅう manjū	PICKLED PLUM 梅干し umeboshi	RICE CAKE 餅 mochi
MISO SOUP みそ汁 miso shiru	JAPANESE SWEETS 和菓子 wagashi	PICKLES 漬け物 tsukemono	RICE CRACKERS せんべい senbei
BOX LUNCH 弁当 bentō	BUCKWHEAT NOODLES そば soba	WHEAT NOODLES そうめん sōmen	INSTANT NOODLES インスタント・ラーメン insutanto rāmen
EKIBEN 駅弁 ekiben	WHEAT NOODLES うどん udon	CHINESE NOODLES ラーメン rāmen	RICE BALL おにぎり onigiri
GRILLED FISH 焼き魚 yakizakana	SUKIYAKI すき焼き sukiyaki	TEMPURA 天ぷら tenpura	SEAWEED のり nori (for onigiri)
GRILLED CHICKEN 焼き鳥 yakitori	PORK CUTLET 豚カツ tonkatsu	BROILED EEL うなぎ unagi	こんぶ konbu (for broth)
BOILED BEEF しゃぶしゃぶ shabu-shabu	SUSHI 寿司 sushi	SLICED RAW FISH 刺身 sashimi	わかめ wakame (for soup)

PROBLEMS

I'm sorry, but I really can't eat this.	Sumimasen ga kore wa taberaremasen.	すみませんがこれは食べられません。
This isn't the food that I ordered.	Chūmon shita mono to chigaimasu.	注文したものと違います。
I didn't order this.	Kore wa chūmon shite imasen.	これは注文していません。
My order hasn't come yet.	Ryōri ga mada kimasen.	料理がまだ来ません。

TASTE 味 aji	**DELICIOUS** おいしい oishii	**OILY** 油っこい aburakkoi	**SOUR** 酸っぱい suppai	**STRONG** (drink) 濃い koi
BITTER 苦い nigai	**HOT, SPICY** 辛い karai	**SALTY** しょっぱい shoppai	**SWEET** 甘い amai	**WEAK (drink)** 薄い usui

PAYING THE BILL

Credit cards like Visa and MasterCard that aren't issued by Japanese banks might not be accepted. American Express and Diner's Club usually present no problems. If planning to use a credit card, carry enough cash just in case.

Often on tables, there are easy-to-miss cylindrical holders into which restaurant bills are often rolled up and stuck. There is no need to leave a tip. There may also be a small device with a button to summon the waiter.

It was delicious.	Oishikatta desu.	おいしかったです。
It was more than I could finish.	Ōsugite nokoshimashita.	多すぎて残しました。
Does the bill include the service charge?	Kono kanjō ni sābisuryō wa fukumarete imasu ka?	この勘定にサービス料は含まれていますか。
Do you accept traveler's checks?	Toraberāzu chekku wa tsukaemasu ka?	トラベラーズチェックは使えますか。
Do you accept credit cards?	Kurejitto kādo wa tsukaemasu ka?	クレジットカードは使えますか。
Excuse me, what is this number/amount for?	Sumimasen ga kore wa nan no kingaku desu ka?	すみませんがこれは何の金額ですか。

124

TABLE THINGS

ASHTRAY 灰皿 haizara	**MATCHES** マッチ matchi	**MOIST HAND TOWEL** おしぼり oshibori	**NAPKIN** ナプキン napukin
JAPANESE WARE 和食器 washokki	**JAPANESE TEAPOT** 急須 kyūsu	**RICE BOWL, TEACUP** 茶碗 chawan	**CHOPSTICKS** 箸 hashi
JAPANESE TEA CUP 湯呑み yunomi	**LACQUER SOUP BOWL** 椀 wan	**TRAY** 盆 bon	**WOODEN CHOPSTICKS** 割り箸 waribashi
WESTERN WARE 洋食器 yōshokki	**DRINKING GLASS** コップ koppu	**DISH, PLATE** 皿 sara	**KNIFE** ナイフ naifu
COFFEE CUP コーヒーカップ kōhii kappu	**GLASS FOR WINE** （ワイン）グラス (wain) gurasu	**FORK** フォーク fōku	**SPOON** スプーン supūn

MISCELLANEOUS VOCABULARY

MORNING SERVICE モーニングサー ビス mōningu sābisu	**APPETIZER** 前菜 zensai	**CAFETERIA** 食堂 shokudō	**DRINK AFTER MEAL** 食後の飲み物 shokugo no nomimono
RESTAURANT レストラン resutoran	**APPETIZER** オードブル ōdoburu	**COFFEE SHOP** 喫茶店 kissaten	**DRINK BEFORE MEAL** 食前酒 shokuzenshu
SET MENU JAPANESE STYLE 定食 teishoku	**SET MENU WESTERN STYLE** セット setto	**MIDNIGHT SNACK** 夜食 yashoku	**RESTAURANT BILL** 勘定 kanjō

LODGING

宿
泊

shukuhaku
lodging

If staying in the city, be prepared to spend a considerable amount of your budget on accommodations. In Tokyo, money that gets a nice and comfortable room elsewhere will get a room barely large enough for a twin bed, refrigerator, television, and an airline-size toilet with shower. There are cheaper alternatives—capsule hotels and *gaijin* houses—cheap boarding houses for foreigners—but both are rarely agreeable.

Depending upon season and location, even high-end hotels and Japanese inns may be noisy by Western standards. Hallways can become common areas, with a lot of traffic among rooms, and, as the evening gets older, commotion sifting out into the hallway. Unlike in the West, where escape to a resort hotel or country inn is a retreat for rest and quiet, in Japan it's often either for a honeymoon or else to let off pressure and stress: a time to party, fueled by drink and friends. On the other hand, again depending on season and location, one might find the most placid of rooms, ghostly quiet save for the sound of one's own breathing. Generally, if at a popular tourist destination, especially during holiday seasons and in summer, you should expect less-than-tranquil conditions.

FINDING A ROOM

I'm looking for some-place to stay tonight. Is any place available?	Tomaru tokoro o sagashite iru n'desu ga dokoka arimasu ka?	泊まるところを探しているんですがどこかありますか。
I'm traveling alone.	Hitori de ryokō shite imasu.	一人で旅行しています。
I'd prefer a ~.	~ ga ii n'desu ga.	～がいいんですが。
western-style hotel	hoteru	ホテル
business hotel	bijinesu hoteru	ビジネスホテル
ryokan	ryokan	旅館
minshuku	minshuku	民宿
capsule hotel	kapuseru hoteru	カプセルホテル
love hotel	rabu hoteru	ラブホテル
youth hostel	yūsu hosuteru	ユースホステル
temple lodging	shukubō	宿坊
gaijin house	gaijin hausu	外人ハウス
I'd like to reserve a room.	Heya o yoyaku shitai n'desu ga.	部屋を予約したいんですが。

How much would you like to spend? ご予算はどのくらいでしょうか。	Do you want a ~? ～がよろしいですか。

Can someone here speak English?	Eigo o hanaseru hito wa imasu ka?	英語を話せる人はいますか。
Do you have a room for tonight?	Konban heya ga arimasu ka?	今晩部屋がありますか。
I don't have a reserva-tion, but is there a room?	Yoyaku shite imasen ga heya wa arimasu ka?	予約していませんが部屋はありますか。
My name is ~.	Watashi wa ~ desu.	私は～です。
I made a reservation.	Yoyaku shimashita.	予約しました。
Here's my confirmation.	Kore ga kakuninsho desu.	これが確認書です。
I'd like to ~ my reserva-tion.	Yoyaku o ~ shitai n'desu ga.	予約を～したいんですが。
confirm	kakunin	確認
cancel	kyanseru	キャンセル
change	henkō	変更
Can you recommend another hotel?	Hoka no hoteru o shōkai shite kuremasen ka?	ほかのホテルを紹介してくれませんか。

PLACES TO STAY

Where to stay? The possibilities are many.

There are the large, INTERNATIONAL-STANDARD HO-TELS, like Hilton and Holiday Inn, offering rooms meeting international expectations. Service is impeccable, as might be expected in Japan, and room prices—room service prices, too—are exorbitant.

An economical version of the Western-style hotel is the BUSINESS HOTEL, a no-frills utilitarian accommodation just adequate for a comfortable night's sleep, perfect for the business traveler. No room service, no porters, no wasted space. Non-smokers will not appreciate the rich and embedded stale cigarette smell.

Not to be outdone for efficiency, the CAPSULE HOTEL takes conservation of space to the absurd, stacking sarcophagus-size compartments on top of one another. One literally crawls in one end, shuts the transparent door, pulls the curtain, and watches a tiny TV or goes to sleep. Designed mostly for businessmen who have missed the last train to the suburbs (or were too drunk to catch it), each capsule holds one person and does not offer much of a night's sleep, unless one is drunk.

LOVE HOTELS are intended for brief romantic appointments, and serve an important role in Japan, where young adults usually live with their parents. Discreet and yet a bit garish, thematic, and sometimes kind of fun, they offer a good night's sleep late at night: beds are big and rooms, soundproof. Better still, decent late-night, all-night rates are available, as they're not much in demand after midnight.

GAIJIN HOUSES offer foreigners communal accommodation in major cities, usually with shared baths and cooking facilities. Often noisy and dirty, they are nevertheless cheap. There are a few decent ones around, but finding them is mostly done through word of mouth.

YOUTH HOSTELS in Japan are, with some exceptions, for travelers who don't mind a little discipline in their lives. With sometimes draconian rules, Japanese hostels offer an injection of group spirit. Even more spartan and somewhat monastic in feel are *shukubō*, or rooms at temples and shrines.

The *RYOKAN* is a Japanese-style inn, usually with impeccable service and often sitting atop a hot spring. For a distinctly Japanese experience, a *ryokan* is unrivaled. Most of them are expensive—the average establishment charges around ¥20,000 per person, and the best places charge upwards of ¥100,000—with futons for sleeping and tatami-floored traditional rooms. Rates are per person, not per room, with two people costing twice as much as one. A full Japanese dinner, exquisitely prepared with local specialties, comes with the room.

More downscale, but equally authentically Japanese, are *MINSHUKU*, which are family-run and much like boarding houses. Rooms are, for Japan, economical, but can be loud, as walls are often thin. Like ryokan, each person pays the same rate, and a Japanese dinner is included.

WESTERN HOTEL ホテル hoteru	**RYOKAN** 旅館 ryokan	**CAPSULE HOTEL** カプセルホテル kapuseru hoteru	**YOUTH HOSTEL** ユースホステル yūsu hosuteru	*GAIJIN* **HOUSE** 外人ハウス gaijin hausu
BUSINESS HOTEL ビジネスホテル bijinesu hoteru	*MINSHUKU* 民宿 minshuku	**LOVE HOTEL** ラブホテル rabu hoteru	**TEMPLE LODGE** 宿坊 shukubō	
BEDDING 寝具 shingu	**SHEET** シーツ shiitsu	**DESK CLERK** フロント係 furonto gakari	**LOBBY** ロビー robii	**SECOND FLOOR** 二階 nikai
BED ベッド beddo	**PILLOW** 枕 makura	**MAID** メード, メイド mēdo, meido	**COFFEE SHOP** コーヒーショップ kōhii shoppu	**STAIRWAYS** 階段 kaidan
FUTON 布団 futon	**NIGHT CLOTHES** 寝巻き nemaki	**MANAGER** 支配人 shihainin	**ELEVATOR** エレベーター erebētā	**EMERGENCY EXIT** 非常口 hijō guchi
BLANKET 毛布 mōfu	**TELEPHONE** 電話 denwa	**BASEMENT** 地下 chika	**FIRST FLOOR** 一階 ikkai	**HOT SPRING** 温泉 onsen

CHECKING IN

Typically, one's bill is based on the number of people who occupied a room, rather than the room itself. Two people will probably pay twice as much as one person. Three people, three times.

Hotels will often have both Western- and Japanese-style rooms. When checking in, you'll inevitably be put in a Western room. You can request a Japanese-style room, but it will be considerably more expensive.

I'd like a ~.	~ o onegai shimasu.	～をお願いします。
quiet room	shizuka-na heya	静かな部屋
room with a nice view	keshiki no ii heya	景色のいい部屋
double room	daburu	ダブル
single room	shinguru	シングル
room for one/two	hitori/futari beya	一人／二人部屋
Does it have a/an ~?	Heya ni wa ~ ga arimasu ka?	部屋には～がありますか。
private bath	o-furo	お風呂
air conditioner	eakon	エアコン
television	terebi	テレビ
I'll stay ~ from tonight.	Konban kara ~ shimasu.	今晩から～します。
one night	ippaku	一泊
two nights	ni-haku	二泊
What is the rate?	Heyadai wa ikura desu ka?	部屋代はいくらですか。
Do you have anything cheaper?	Motto yasui heya wa arimasen ka?	もっと安い部屋はありませんか。

How much would you like to spend? ご予算はどのくらいでしょうか。	**We have only singles/doubles.** 一人／二人用の部屋しかありません。
Yes, we have a room. ええ、あります。	**We're full tonight.** 今夜は満室です。
How long do you plan to stay? 宿泊のご予定は。	**We're full all week.** 今週はずっと満室です。

CHECKING IN

How much is ~?	~ ikura desu ka?	～いくらですか。
it altogether	zenbu de	全部で
a single room	shinguru wa	シングルは
a double room	daburu wa	ダブルは
the service charge	sābisuryō wa	サービス料は
Are service charges included?	Sābisuryōkomi desu ka?	サービス料込みですか。
Are there any additional expenses or costs?	Nanika betsu ni hiyō ga kakarimasu ka?	何かべつに費用がかかりますか。
Does the price include breakfast/lunch/dinner?	Chōshoku/Chūshoku/Yūshoku-tsuki no nedan desu ka?	朝食／昼食／夕食付きの値段ですか。
I'd like to pay by credit card.	Kurejitto kādo de onegai shimasu.	クレジットカードでお願いします。
Do you accept credit cards?	Kurejitto kādo wa tsukae-masu ka?	クレジットカードは使えますか
Do you take traveler's checks?	Toraberāzu chekku wa tsukaemasu ka?	トラベラーズチェックは使えますか。
Is there room service?	Rūmu sābisu ga arimasu ka?	ルームサービスがありますか。
Is there laundry service?	Sentaku no sābisu ga arimasu ka?	洗濯のサービスがありますか。
Is there dry cleaning service?	Dorai kuriiningu no sābisu ga arimasu ka?	ドライクリーニングのサービスがありますか。
When is check-out time?	Chekku auto wa nan ji desu ka?	チェックアウトは何時ですか。
Can I get a late check-out?	Chekku auto o osoku deki-masu ka?	チェックアウトを遅くできますか。
Can I get the room right now?	Heya wa ima sugu toremasu ka?	部屋は今すぐとれますか。
Can I go to the room now?	Ima sugu heya ni hairemasu ka?	今すぐ部屋に入れますか。

The price includes breakfast/lunch/dinner.
朝食／昼食／夕食付きの値段です。

Do you have luggage?
荷物はありますか。

We don't take credit cards.
クレジットカードは受けつけていません。

The room isn't ready yet.
まだ部屋の用意ができていません。

We don't take traveler's checks.
トラベラーズチェックは受けつけていません。

The room will be realty at ~.
～時には部屋をご利用いただけます。

DURING THE STAY

English	Romaji	Japanese
Can I check my valuable things?	Kichōhin o azukatte moraemasu ka?	貴重品を預かってもらえますか。
Can I keep this/these in your safe?	Kore o kinko ni azukatte moraemasu ka?	これを金庫に預かってもらえますか。
I'd like to get my things from your safe.	Kinko ni azuketa mono o dashitai n'desu ga.	金庫に預けたものを出したいんですが。
I'd like to send a fax.	Fakkusu o okuritai n'desu ga.	ファックスを送りたいんですが。
What's the fax number here?	Fakkusu bangō wa nan ban desu ka?	ファックス番号は何番ですか。
Are there any messages for me?	Watashi ate no dengon ga todoite imasu ka?	私あての伝言が届いていますか。
I'd like a card with the hotel's address.	Kono hoteru no jūsho o kaita kādo o kudasai.	このホテルの住所を書いたカードを下さい。
Where is the nearest subway station?	Koko kara ichiban chikai chikatetsu no eki wa doko desu ka?	ここから一番近い地下鉄の駅はどこですか。
I'd like a wakeup call at ~.	~ ji ni okoshite kudasai.	～時に起こして下さい。
I'd like it taken to my room.	Heya ni motte kite hoshii n'desu ga.	部屋に持って来てほしいんですが。
Please send ~ to my room.	~ o heya ni todokete kudasai.	～を部屋に届けて下さい。
soap	sekken	せっけん
towels	taoru	タオル
toilet paper	toiretto pēpā	トイレットペーパー
blanket	mōfu	毛布
ice	kōri	氷
Can you hold this luggage for me?	Kono nimotsu o azukatte moraemasu ka?	この荷物を預かってもらえますか。
I'd like to send this baggage to ~ by delivery service.	Kono nimotsu o ~ e okuritai n'desu ga.	この荷物を～へ送りたいんですが。
I'd like you to come get it for me.	Tori ni kite hoshii n'desu ga.	取りに来てほしいんですが。
Please don't disturb me.	Okosanai de kudasai.	起こさないで下さい。
Please make up this room.	Heya o sōji shite kudasai.	部屋を掃除して下さい。
Who is it?	Dare desu ka?	誰ですか。
One moment, please.	Chotto matte kudasai.	ちょっと待って下さい。
Please come in.	Dōzo.	どうぞ。

TELEPHONE

Modern hotels will have direct dial lines, but older hotels may require use of a switchboard. *Ryokan* and *minshuku* almost never have phones in rooms. If you're at a deluxe hotel, various departments, like room service and laundry, will understand enough English to manage your requests or queries. Just make sure to speak slowly, and clearly.

I'd like extension ~.	Naisen ~ o onegai shimasu.	内線〜をお願いします。
I'd like room service.	Rūmu sābisu o onegai shimasu.	ルームサービスをお願いします。
I'd like the front desk.	Furonto o onegai shimasu.	フロントをお願いします。
I'd like to call ~.	~ o onegai shimasu.	〜をお願いします。
I'd like to make a long-distance call.	Chōkyori denwa o onegai shimasu.	長距離電話をお願いします。
This is a collect call.	Korekuto kōru de onegai shimasu.	コレクトコールでお願いします。
This is a credit card call.	Kurejitto kādo kōru de onegai shimasu.	クレジットカードコールでお願いします。
May I speak in English?	Eigo de hanashite ii desu ka?	英語で話していいですか。
Sorry, I don't understand.	Sumimasen ga wakarimasen.	すみませんが分かりません。

HOT TIME IN THE ONSEN

The Japanese love getting into hot water. Japan is peppered with hot springs, or *onsen*, and except for those in the remote wilderness, most hot springs have been developed into resorts.

Visiting an *onsen* is a unique experience. For a foreigner, the experience can be both pleasant and uncomfortable at the same time. If you've been stared at on the street, imagine the stares when you're naked at a rural hot spring resort. But soaking in an *onsen*, Japanese-style, is a pleasure. And afterwards, you can do as the Japanese do and take an evening stroll in *yukata* and sandals.

In the *onsen*, one soaks and communes with friends or nature. Don't take soap into the water with you. Washing is done beforehand while sitting on a stool in a row of hand-held showers and mirrors. Wash, then rinse off completely—taking care not to splatter your neighbor—before entering the *onsen*. Note that water in the *onsen* is very, very hot.

PROBLEMS

As elsewhere in Asia, displays of anger and indignant demands for action are neither respected nor effective in Japan. But rarely will you need to make a complaint more than once. Service is usually prompt and done with a smile.

Would you get the manager, please?	Shihainin o yonde kudasai.	支配人を呼んで下さい。
I left the key in my room.	Heya ni kagi o okiwasuremashita.	部屋に鍵を置き忘れました。
I've lost my room key.	Kagi o nakushite shimaimashita.	鍵をなくしてしまいました。
Can I change rooms?	Heya o kaete moraemasu ka?	部屋を変えてもらえますか。
I'd like to change rooms.	Heya o kaetai n'desu ga.	部屋を変えたいんですが。
Is there a larger room?	Motto ōkii heya ga arimasu ka?	もっと大きい部屋がありますか。
Is there a better room?	Mō sukoshi ii heya ga arimasu ka?	もう少しいい部屋がありますか。
Is there a quiet room?	Shizuka-na heya ga arimasu ka?	静かな部屋がありますか。
It's too small.	Chotto chiisasugimasu.	ちょっと小さすぎます。
It's too noisy.	Chotto yakamashisugimasu.	ちょっとやかましすぎます。
The bathtub doesn't drain.	Furo no mizu ga demasen.	風呂の水が出ません。
The lock is broken.	Kagi ga kowarete imasu.	鍵がこわれています。
The television doesn't work.	Terebi ga tsukimasen.	テレビがつきません。
The telephone isn't working.	Denwa ga kowarete imasu.	電話がこわれています。
The toilet doesn't flush.	Toire no mizu ga nagaremasen.	トイレの水が流れません。
There's no hot water.	Oyu ga demasen.	お湯が出ません。
There's no soap/towel.	Sekken/Taoru ga arimasen.	せっけん／タオルがありません。
The ~ doesn't work.	~ ga kowarete imasu.	～がこわれています。
air conditioner	eakon	エアコン
electric fan	senpūki	扇風機
heater	danbō	暖房
electricity	denki	電気
radio	rajio	ラジオ
television	terebi	テレビ
window	mado	窓
key/lock	kagi	鍵

CHECKING OUT

No mysteries here. Checking out means paying the bill. As a rule, *ryokan* and *minshuku* don't take credit cards. Most Western-style hotels will take some type of card, but not necessarily all cards. American Express offers a listing of Japanese-style lodgings accepting AmEx.

I'd like to check out ~.	~ chekku auto shitai n'desu ga.	〜チェックアウトしたいんですが。
soon	sugu ni	すぐに
around noon	hiru goro	昼頃
early tomorrow	ashita hayaku	明日早く
tomorrow morning	ashita no asa	明日の朝
I'm checking out.	Ima chekku auto shimasu.	今チェックアウトします。
I'd like to leave a day early.	Ichi nichi hayaku tachitai n'desu ga.	一日早く発ちたいんですが。
I'd like to stay an extra day.	Mō ippaku shitai n'desu ga.	もう一泊したいんですが。
I'd like to stay longer.	Taizai o nobashitai n'desu ga.	滞在を延ばしたいんですが。
My bill, please.	Shiharai o onegai shimasu.	支払をお願いします。
There may be an error on the bill.	Seikyūsho ni machigai ga aru yō desu ga.	請求書に間違いがあるようですが。
Can you check it again?	Sumimasen ga mō ichido tashikamete kudasai.	すみませんがもう一度確かめて下さい。
I'd like to get my luggage.	Azuketa nimotsu o dashitai n'desu ga.	預けた荷物を出したいんですが。
I'd like to store my luggage.	Kono nimotsu o azukatte kudasai.	この荷物を預かって下さい。
Please call a taxi.	Takushii o yonde kudasai.	タクシーを呼んで下さい。

That will/will not be a problem.
それは困ります／かまいません。

The bill and charges are correct.
間違いはありません。

How much longer do you wish to stay?
どれくらい滞在を延ばされますか。

When will you return for your luggage?
荷物はいつ引き取りますか。

Getting Along
LEISURE

余暇

yoka
leisure time

It's difficult to become bored in Japan. There's too much to tease the senses and surprise the intellect.

Walk through Tokyo's Shinjuku or Ikebukuro districts at night, and just how seriously the Japanese take entertainment becomes clear. Most towns and cities have smaller versions of these areas. Pachinko parlors, bright and smoky places of clamoring pinball machines and seemingly dazed players, are abundant. Small cafes and coffee boutiques, usually themed in some way, offer cramped solitude and good, though expensive, thimbles of coffee. Adult entertainment barkers stand amidst bright pink and purple lights. On the periphery, not-so-subtle love hotels beckon couples with a yen.

On the tourist agenda, Shinjuku is the night life by which all others are measured: brassy, loud, electric. More traditional is the entertainment of Ginza: sophisticated and discreet, understated and expensive. A walk through each unveils a different texture of Japanese relaxation.

In the end, most of us want something more modest, like a movie, a baseball game. or even a kabuki performance— or at least one act, as they last for hours.

SOMETHING TO DO

Entertainment is expensive, movies costing at least twice the price of films in Europe or North America. Check one of the English-language daily newspapers for a listing of what's going on in Tokyo. *Tokyo Journal* contains more extensive entertainment listings.

I want to see ~.	~ o mitai n'desu ga.	～を見たいんですが。
I'd like to go see ~.	~ o mi ni ikitai n'desu ga.	～を見にいきたいんですが。
Where can I see ~?	~ wa doko de miraremasu ka?	～はどこで見られますか。
Would you like to see ~ with me?	Issho ni ~ o mi ni ikimasen ka?	一緒に～を見にいきませんか。
judo	jūdō	柔道
karate	karate	空手
kendo	kendō	剣道
a baseball game	yakyū/bēsubōru no shiai	野球／ベースボールの試合
kabuki	kabuki	歌舞伎
noh	nō	能
sumo	sumō	相撲
a concert	ongakkai	音楽会
a movie	eiga	映画
a drama/play	engeki	演劇
a play	geki	劇
I'd like to try pachinko.	Pachinko o yatte mitai desu.	パチンコをやってみたいです。
Where can one see Japanese flower arrangement?	Ikebana o miru ni wa doko e ikeba ii desu ka?	生け花を見るにはどこへ行けばいいですか。
Where can one see a Japanese tea ceremony?	Sadō o miru ni wa doko e ikeba ii desu ka?	茶道を見るにはどこへ行けばいいですか。

Do you know when it is?	Sore wa itsu ka gozonji desu ka?	それはいつかごぞんじですか。
What time does the ~ show begin?	~ no kai wa nanji ni hajimarimasu ka?	～の回は何時に始まりますか。
first	saisho	最初
last	saigo	最後
What time does the show/performance begin?	Kaien wa nan ji desu ka?	開演は何時ですか。

13

GETTING ALONG

What time does the show/performance end?	Shūen wa nan ji desu ka?	終演は何時ですか。
What time does the movie start?	Eiga wa nan ji kara desu ka?	映画は何時からですか。
What time does the movie finish?	Eiga wa nan ji made desu ka?	映画は何時までですか。
It continues until (*time*).	~ wa (jikan) made desu.	～は (時間) までです。
It starts from (*time*).	~ wa (jikan) kara desu.	～は (時間) からです。
It's already started.	Mō hajimatte imasu.	もう始まっています。

Do you know where the ~ is?	~ wa doko ka gozonji desu ka?	～はどこかごぞんじですか。
movie theater	eigakan	映画館
concert hall	konsāto hōru	コンサートホール
theater	gekijō	劇場
stage	butai	舞台
Is there an admission charge?	Nyūjōryō wa irimasu ka?	入場料はいりますか。
What is the admission charge?	Nyūjōryō wa ikura desu ka?	入場料はいくらですか。
I'd like to reserve seats.	Seki o yoyaku shitai n'desu ga.	席を予約したいんですが。
adult	otona	大人
child	kodomo	子供
advance ticket	maeuriken	前売り券
entrance fee	nyūjōryō	入場料
reserved seating	shiteiseki	指定席
open/free seating	jiyūseki	自由席
audience seat	kyakuseki	客席
Please show me my seat.	Seki ni annai shite kudasai.	席に案内して下さい。

ACTOR 俳優 haiyū	AUDIENCE 観客 kankyaku	COMEDY 喜劇 kigeki	HORROR ホラー horā	SCIENCE FICTION SF esu efu
ACTOR 役者 yakusha	SUBTITLE 字幕 jimaku	HISTORICAL 歴史物 rekishimono	MYSTERY ミステリー misuterii	TRAGEDY 悲劇 higeki

INTERESTS AND ACTIVITIES

If you get into a conversation, whether English or Japanese, inevitably you'll be asked about your hobbies. To a Japanese person, "hobbies" means interests like skiing and golfing, not necessarily stamp or bug collecting.

What are your hobbies?	Shumi wa nan desu ka?	趣味は何ですか。
What do you like to do?	Nani o suru no ga suki desu ka?	何をするのが好きですか。
I have an interest in ~.	~ ni kyōmi ga arimasu.	～に興味があります。
I love to ~.	~ ga daisuki desu.	～が大好きです。
I hate to ~.	~ wa kirai desu.	～は嫌いです。
I want to study ~.	~ o benkyō shitai desu.	～を勉強したいです。
I'd like to try ~.	~ o yatte mitai desu.	～をやってみたいです。
I want to do ~.	~ o shitai n'desu ga.	～をしたいんですが。
I like to watch ~.	~ o miru no ga suki desu.	～をみるのが好きです。
Would you like to ~?	~ o shitai desu ka?	～をしたいですか。
I like to do ~.	~ o suru no ga suki desu.	～をするのが好きです。
architecture	kenchiku	建築
art	bijutsu	美術
calligraphy	shodō	書道
card games	toranpu	トランプ
ceramics	yakimono	焼き物
chess, Japanese	shōgi	将棋
dance	odori	踊り
film, Japanese	Nihon no eiga	日本の映画
flower arrangement	ikebana	生け花
folk art	mingei	民芸
games	gēmu	ゲーム
gardens, Japanese	Nihon teien	日本庭園
painting, Japanese	Nihon ga	日本画
photography	shashin	写真
pottery	yakimono	焼き物
reading	dokusho	読書
sculpture	chōkoku	朝食
sightseeing	kankō	観光
travel	ryokō	旅行

SPORTS

SPORTS スポーツ supōtsu	BOATING ボート bōto	HIKING ハイキング haikingu	MOUNTAIN CLIMBING 登山 tozan	SWIMMING 水泳 suiei
AIKIDO 合気道 aikidō	FISHING 釣り tsuri	HORSERIDING 乗馬 jōba	RACE レース rēsu	TABLE TENNIS 卓球 takkyū
ARCHERY 弓道 kyūdō	FOOTBALL, US フットボール futtobōru	JUDO 柔道 jūdō	SKATING スケート sukēto	TENNIS テニス tenisu
BASEBALL 野球 yakyū	GOLF ゴルフ gorufu	KARATE 空手 karate	SKIING スキー sukii	TRACK AND FIELD 陸上競技 rikujō kyōgi
BASKETBALL バスケットボ ール basuketto bōru	GYMNASTICS 体操 taisō	KENDO 剣道 kendō	SOCCER サッカー sakkā	WATER SPORTS 水上スポーツ suijō supōtsu
BICYCLING サイクリング saikuringu	HANG GLIDING ハングライ ダー hangu guraidā	MARATHON マラソン marason	SUMO 相撲 sumō	WIND SURFING ウィンドサー フィン uindosāfin

ESSENTIAL VERBS

to participate in
参加する
sanka suru

to exercise
運動する
undō suru

to win
勝つ
katsu

to compete
競争する
kyōsō suru

to practice, train
稽古する
keiko suru

to lose
負ける
makeru

READING

Who is your favorite ~?	Suki-na ~ wa dare desu ka?	好きな～は誰ですか。
author	sakka	作家
novelist	shōsetsuka	小説家
poet	shijin	詩人
writer	sakka	作家
I like to read ~.	~ o yomu no ga suki desu.	～を読むのが好きです。

LITERATURE 文学 bungaku	ESSAYS エッセー essē	HISTORY 歴史 rekishi	LOVE STORIES 恋愛小説 ren'ai shōsetsu	OLD STORIES 昔話 mukashi banashi
BIOGRAPHIES 伝記 denki	FAIRY TALES 童話 dōwa	HORROR ホラー horā	MYSTERIES ミステリー misuterii	POETRY 詩 shi
CLASSICAL LITERATURE 古典文学 koten bungaku	HISTORICAL DRAMAS 歴史劇 rekishigeki	LEGENDS 伝説 densetsu	MYTHS 神話 shinwa	SCIENCE FICTION SF esu efu

ARTS

I like to visit/go to ~.	~ e iku no ga suki desu.	～へ行くのが好きです。
museums	hakubutsukan	博物館
displays, exhibitions	tenrankai	展覧会
I like to look at ~.	~ o miru no ga suki desu.	～見るのが好きです。
I like to do ~.	~ o suru no ga suki desu.	～をするのが好きです。

ART 芸術 geijutsu	CERAMICS 焼き物 yakimono	FOLK ART 民芸 mingei	PHOTOGRAPHY 写真 shashin	ARTIST 芸術家 geijutsuka
CALLIGRAPHY 書道 shodō	FINE ARTS 美術 bijutsu	PAINTINGS 絵, 絵画 e, kaiga	SCULPTURE 彫刻 chōkoku	PAINTER 画家 gaka

MUSIC

I like listening to ~.	~ o kiku no ga suki desu.	～を聴くのが好きです。
I like playing ~ (piano, guitar).	~ o hiku no ga suki desu.	～を弾くのが好きです。
I like playing ~ (trumpet, flute).	~ o fuku no ga suki desu.	～を吹くのが好きです。

MUSIC 音楽 ongaku	CONCERT コンサート konsāto	SINGER 歌手 kashu	JAZZ ジャズ jazu	CLASSICAL MUSIC クラシック kurashikku
INSTRUMENT 楽器 gakki	SONG 歌 uta	MUSICIAN 音楽家 ongakuka	LATIN MUSIC ラテン音楽 raten ongaku	ROCK AND ROLL ロック rokku
PERFOR-MANCE 演奏 ensō	ORCHESTRA オーケストラ ōkesutora	FOLK SONGS 民謡 min'yō	POPULAR MUSIC ポップス poppusu	KARAOKE カラオケ karaoke

ESSENTIAL VERBS

to appreciate, enjoy 鑑賞する kanshō suru	to walk, stroll 散歩する sanpo suru	to display, exhibit 展示する tenji suru
to be impressed 感動する kandō suru	to play an instrument 演奏する ensō suru	to draw, paint 描く kaku
to enjoy 楽しむ tanoshimu	to sing a song 歌を歌う uta o utau	to sculpt 彫刻する chōkoku suru
to travel 旅行する ryokō suru	to learn, to take lessons 習う narau	to write, to publish 著す arawasu

NATIONAL HOLIDAYS

New Year's Day	**Constitution Day**	**Autumnal Equinox Day**
1 January	**3 May**	**around 23 September***
元日	憲法記念日	秋分の日
Ganjitsu	Kenpō Kinenbi	Shūbun no hi
Coming-of-Age Day	**Greenery Day**	**Sports Day**
2nd Monday of January	**4 May**	**2nd Mon. of October**
成人の日	みどりの日	体育の日
Seijin no hi	Midori no hi	Taiiku no hi
National Foundation Day	**Children's Day**	**Culture Day**
11 February	**5 May**	**3 November**
建国記念の日	こどもの日	文化の日
Kenkoku Kinen no hi	Kodomo no hi	Bunka no hi
Vernal Equinox Day	**Marine Day**	**Labor Thanksgiving Day**
Around 21 March*	**3rd Monday of July**	**23 November**
春分の日	海の日	勤労感謝の日
Shūnbun no hi	Umi no hi	Kinro Kansha no hi
Showa Day	**Respect-for-Aged Day**	**Emperor's Birthday**
29 April	**3rd Monday of September**	**23 December**
昭和の日	敬老の日	天皇誕生日
Shōwa no hi	Keirō no hi	Tennō Tanjōbi

* The precise dates of the vernal and autumnal equinoxes change from year to year.

TRAVEL SEASONS

There are a few weeks each year when seemingly the entire population of Japan is on vacation. Companies close down, subways are empty in the cities, and trains and highways leading from main urban areas are packed. They are: New Year's, from around 28 December to 4 January; Golden Week, from 29 April to around 5 May; Bon festival, from around 15 August for one or two weeks; and July and August, especially late August.

PROBLEMS

病
気

byōki
illness

Problems
ILLNESS

It's a hassle getting sick when traveling. But if you do, medical facilities are excellent in Japan, with high levels of care. For really esoteric diagnoses and treatments, however, Japan's health care establishment is rather conservative.

If consulting a Japanese doctor, you should know that Japan's medical tradition and system allow him or her to choose to tell you nothing about your diagnosis and treatment. The doctor need not say what's wrong, or explain the many bottles of medicine s/he will often prescribe. It is not unusual for a doctor to withhold information from a patient, if s/he feels that knowledge of a condition—terminal cancer is one example— would be upsetting.

A Japanese patient will usually accept a doctor's orders and do unquestioningly whatever s/he is told to do. The patient who does question a doctor, even out of benign curiosity, risks being considered disrespectful and untrusting.

Although Japan has a comprehensive national health care system, if you are a nonresident and thus not participating in the system, you will be financially responsible for all treatment.

GETTING HELP

There are three options should you need a doctor. If at a first-class hotel, you can utilize the house physician at premium prices. Or, you can go to a public hospital or clinic, and be prepared for a long wait (2 to 3 hours is not uncommon) and possible problems with language. Otherwise, in major cities, you can go to one of the several private clinics staffed by Western physicians. For many people, it can be more comfortable talking about health problems in one's own language.

Call for a doctor, please.	Isha o yonde kudasai.	医者を呼んで下さい。
Take me to the hospital.	Byōin e tsurete itte kudasai.	病院へ連れて行って下さい。
Do you know an English-speaking doctor?	Eigo o hanaseru isha o shitte imasu ka?	英語を話せる医者を知っていますか？
I need an interpreter.	Tsūyaku ga hitsuyō desu.	通訳が必要です。

SYMPTOMS

It hurts here.	Koko ga itamimasu.	ここが痛みます。
sharp pain	Kiri-kiri itamimasu.	きりきり痛みます。
not sharp, but continuous	Shiku-shiku itamimasu.	しくしく痛みます。
when you press hard	Tsuyoku osu to itamimasu.	つよく押すと痛みます。
when you press softly	Chotto oshita dake de tamimasu.	ちょっと押しただけで痛みます。
even when not touched	Nanimo shinakute mo itamimasu.	何もしなくても痛みます。
The pain comes and goes.	Toki-doki itamimasu.	ときどき痛みます。
I've had the pain since ~.	~ kara itami ga arimasu.	～から痛みがあります。
this morning	kesa	今朝
yesterday	kinō	昨日
the day before yesterday	ototoi	おととい
last week	senshū	先週
I feel sick.	Kibun ga warui desu.	気分が悪いです。
I feel nauseous.	Hakike ga shimasu.	吐き気がします。
I have a ~.	~ o hikimashita.	～をひきました。
cold	kaze	風邪
chest cold	seki no deru kaze	せきの出る風邪
head cold	hana kaze	鼻風邪

PROBLEMS

I have a headache.	Atama ga itai desu.	頭が痛いです。
I have sharp pain.	Kiri-kiri itamimasu.	きりきり痛みます。
I have throbbing pain.	Zuki-zuki itamimasu.	ずきずき痛みます。
I've got a temperature.	Netsu ga arimasu.	熱があります。
I feel dizzy.	Memai ga shimasu.	めまいがします。
I have a chill.	Samuke ga shimasu.	寒気がします。
I have a cough.	Seki ga demasu.	せきが出ます。
I have a sore throat.	Nodo ga itai desu.	のどが痛いです。
I have a stomachache.	I ga itai desu.	胃が痛いです。
I've got diarrhea.	Geri desu.	下痢です。
I'm constipated.	Benpi desu.	便秘です。
My chest hurts.	Mune ga kurushii desu.	胸が苦しいです。
I've got a toothache.	Ha ga itai desu.	歯が痛いです。
I'm sleepy.	Nemui desu.	眠いです。
I'm tired.	Tsukaremashita.	疲れました。
I've got a poor appetite.	Shokuyoku ga arimasen.	食欲がありません。

SYMPTOMS 症状 shōjō	DIZZINESS めまい memai	ITCHY かゆい kayui	PERSPIRE 汗をかく ase o kaku	TOOTHACHE 歯痛 haita
CHILL 寒気 samuke	FEVER 熱 netsu	LACK OF SLEEP 睡眠不足 suimin busoku	RUNNY NOSE 鼻が出る hana ga deru	TOOTH CAVITY 虫歯の穴 mushiba no ana
CONSTIPA-TION 便秘 benpi	HANGOVER 二日酔い futsukayoi	NAUSEA 吐き気 hakike	NASAL MUCUS 鼻水 hana mizu	VOMIT 吐く haku
COUGH せき seki	HEADACHE 頭痛 zutsū	PAIN 痛み itami	STOMACH-ACHE 腹痛 fukutsū	RINGING IN EARS 耳鳴り miminari
DIARRHEA 下痢 geri	INDIGESTION 食あたり shokuatari	HURTS 痛い itai	SWELLING できもの dekimono	LOSE WEIGHT 痩せる yaseru

Illness

EXAMINATION

For Westerners used to frank discussions with their doctor, not to mention getting a second opinion when in doubt, the Japanese doctor's expectation of blind trust—and the aloofness of many doctors themselves— can be maddening.

Where were you before Japan? 日本に来る前はどこにいましたか。	**I want a ~ sample.** 〜検査をします。
Have you had this problem before? 前に同じ症状になったことがありますか。	**blood** 血液
What kinds of medicine are you taking? どんな薬を飲んでいますか。	**urine** 尿
I'll take your temperature. 体温を計ります。	**stool** 便
I'll take your blood pressure. 血圧を計ります。	**I'm going to take an x-ray.** レントゲンをとります。

HEALTH 健康 kenkō	CHECKUP 健康診断 kenkō shindan	TEST 検査 kensa	BLOOD 血, 血液 chi, ketsueki	INJECTION 注射 chūsha
CONDITION 具合 guai	INITIAL EXAM 初診 shoshin	CURE 治療 chiryō	BLOOD PRESSURE 血圧 ketsuatsu	OPERATION 手術 shujutsu
TO EXAMINE 診察する shinsatsu suru	MEDICAL EXAM 診察 shinsatsu	PULSE 脈拍 myakuhaku	BLOOD TYPE 血液型 ketsuekigata	VACCINATION 予防注射 yobō chūsha
GET SICK 病気になる byōki ni naru	TREATMENT 治療 chiryō	BODY TEMPERATURE 体温 taion	DISINFECTION 消毒 shōdoku	EXAMINATION ROOM 診察室 shinsatsushitsu

THE BODY

THE BODY	FOREHEAD	EYE	CHEEK	TONGUE
体	額	目	頬	舌
karada	hitai	me	hō	shita
HEAD	FACE	EYEBALL	NOSE	TOOTH
頭	顔	眼球／目玉	鼻	歯
atama	kao	gankyū/medama	hana	ha
BRAIN	TEMPLE	EYEBROW	MOUTH	JAW, CHIN
脳	こめかみ	まゆ毛	口	あご
nō	komekami	mayuge	kuchi	ago
HAIR	EAR	EYELASH	LIP	NECK
髪の毛	耳	まつ毛	くちびる	首
kami no ke	mimi	matsuge	kuchibiru	kubi

TORSO	SHOULDER	SIDE	CHEST, BREAST	HIP, WAIST
胴	肩	脇腹	胸	腰
dō	kata	yoko bara	mune	koshi
RIB	ARMPIT	BACK	BELLY	BUTTOCKS
肋骨	わきの下	背中	おなか	おしり
rokkotsu	waki no shita	senaka	o-naka	o-shiri

INTERNAL	MUSCLE	ESOPHAGUS	LUNG	STOMACH
内蔵	筋肉	食道	肺	胃
naizō	kinniku	shokudō	hai	i
BLOOD	SKIN	HEART	INTESTINES	GENITALS
血、血液	皮膚	心臓	腸	生殖器
chi, ketsueki	hifu	shinzō	chō	seishokuki
BONE	THROAT	LIVER	KIDNEY	UTERUS
骨	のど	肝臓	腎臓	子宮
hone	nodo	kanzō	jinzō	shikyū

EXTREMITIES	WRIST	FINGERNAIL	KNEE	FOOT
手足	手首	爪	ひざ	足
te ashi	te kubi	tsume	hiza	ashi
JOINT	**HAND**	**FINGERPRINT**	**SHIN**	**HEEL**
関節	手	指紋	すね	かかと
kansetsu	te	shimon	sune	kakato
ARM	**THUMB**	**LEG**	**CALF**	**TOE**
腕	親指	脚	ふくらはぎ	つま先
ude	oya yubi	ashi	fukura hagi	tsumasaki
ELBOW	**FINGER**	**THIGH**	**ANKLE**	**NERVE**
ひじ	指	太もも	足首	神経
hiji	yubi	futomomo	ashi kubi	shinkei

PHYSICAL INJURIES

I fell and hit my ~.	Koronde ~ o uchimashita.	転んで～をうちました。
My ~ hurts.	~ ga itai desu.	～が痛いです。
It hurts when I move it.	Ugokasu to itamimasu.	動かすと痛みます。

BLEEDING	BRUISE	CUT, GASH	LUMP, BUMP	SPRAIN
出血	打ち身	切り傷	こぶ	ねんざ
shukketsu	uchimi	kirikizu	kobu	nenza
BONE FRACTURE	**BURN**	**INTERNAL BLEEDING**	**SCRATCH**	**WOUND**
骨折	やけど	内出血	かすり傷	傷
kossetsu	yakedo	naishukketsu	kasurikizu	kizu

DIAGNOSIS

As noted previously, Japanese doctors often withhold information from patients. To question a doctor about diagnosis and treatment is to show irreverence and lack of trust.

On the other hand, the fact that you're a foreigner may give the doctor license to be more candid with you.

| I'm a diabetic. | Watashi wa tōnyōbyō desu. | 私は糖尿病です。 |
| I have an allergy to ~. | ~ ni arerugii ga arimasu. | 〜にアレルギーがあります。 |

It's broken. 折れています。	I'm giving you antibiotics. 抗生物質を処方します。
It's sprained. ねんざしています。	You should go to the hospital for tests. 検査のために病院へ行って下さい。
It's infected. 化膿しています。	I want you to come back in ~ days. 〜日間たったらまた来て下さい。
I believe that it's ~. 〜だと思います。	Are you allergic to any medicines? 薬のアレルギーはありますか。

I think that you should go to the hospital for treatment.
治療のために病院へ行って下さい。

ALLERGY アレルギー arerugii	COMMON COLD 普通の風邪 futsū no kaze	HEART ATTACK 心臓発作 shizō hossa	MEASLES はしか hashika	PREGNANCY 妊娠 ninshin
APPENDICITIS 盲腸炎 mōchō	FATIGUE 疲れ tsukare	HEPATITIS 肝炎 kan'en	MISCARRIAGE 流産 ryūzan	RASH 発疹 hosshin
CANCER がん gan	FOOD POISONING 食中毒 shokūchudoku	INFECTION 伝染病 densenbyō	PNEUMONIA 肺炎 haien	URINARY INFECTION 尿道炎 nyōdōen
COLD, FLU 風邪 kaze	HAY FEVER 花粉症 kafunshō	INFLUENZA インフルエンザ infuruenza	POISONING 中毒 chūdoku	

MEDICINES

Japanese doctors often prescribe mountains of pills. Unfortunately, you may have no idea what they are, whether they be antibiotics or vitamins (commonly prescribed for illnesses). For minor ailments, there are over-the-counter medicines. Tell the pharmacist or drugstore clerk your problem, and s/he'll steer you to the right medicine.

Please fill this prescription.	Kono shohōsen de kusuri o kudasai.	この処方せんで薬を下さい。
I need medicine for ~.	~ no kusuri o kudasai.	～の薬を下さい。
I'd like some ~.	~ o kudasai.	～を下さい。

BEFORE MEALS 食前 shokuzen	**COLD** 風邪 kaze	**CONSTIPA- TION** 便秘 benpi	**FEVER** 熱 netsu	**HEADACHE** 頭痛 zutsū
AFTER MEALS 食後 shokugo	**COUGH** せき seki	**DIARRHEA** 下痢 geri	**HAY FEVER** 花粉症 kafunshō	**UPSET STOMACH** 胃のもたれ i no motare
ANTIBIOTIC 抗生物質 kōseibusshitsu	**HERBAL MEDICINE** 漢方薬 kanpōyaku	**DIARRHEA MEDICINE** 下痢止め geridome	**HEADACHE MEDICINE** 頭痛薬 zutsūyaku	**OINTMENT** 軟膏 nankō
ANTISEPTIC 消毒薬 shōdokuyaku	**COLD MEDICINE** 風邪薬 kaze gusuri	**EYEDROPS** 目薬 me gusuri	**LAXATIVE** 下剤 gezai	**SLEEPING PILL** 睡眠薬 suiminyaku
ASPIRIN アスピリン asupirin	**COUGH MEDICINE** せき止め sekidome	**FEVER MEDICINE** 解熱剤 genetsuzai	**PAIN KILLER** 痛み止め itamidome	**STOMACH MEDICINE** 胃薬 igusuri
PHARMACY 薬局 yakkyoku	**MEDICINE** 薬 kusuri	**PRESCRIP- TION** 処方せん shohōsen	**PILL, TABLET** 錠剤 jōzai	**INTERNAL MEDICINE** 飲み薬 nomigusuri

THE HOSPITAL

If you're to be hospitalized, don't panic. It may not be serious after all. Colds and influenza are regularly treated with hospitalization in Japan, as is fatigue. Japanese doctors frequently order hospitalization for illnesses that doctors in other countries might treat more lightly, even with over-the-counter drugs. Moreover, the length of the average hospital stay in Japan is three to six times that in Europe or North America. Not so bad if you're overworked, stressed out, tired of everything, and not paying for the stay, especially for the overworked *sarariman* who takes too few vacations.

I'm going to send you to a specialist. 専門医のところへ行ってもらいます。

CARDIOLOGY 循環器科 junkankika	GYNECOLOGY 婦人科 fujinka	NEUROSUR-GERY 神経外科 shinkei geka	ORTHOPEDICS 整形外科 seikei geka	UROLOGY 泌尿器科 hinyōkika
DENTISTRY 歯科 shika	INTERNAL MEDICINE 内科 naika	OBSTETRICS 産科 sanka	PEDIATRICS 小児科 shōnika	EAR/NOSE/THROAT 耳鼻咽喉科 jibiinkōka
DERMATOLOGY 皮膚科 hifuka	NEUROLOGY 神経科 shinkeika	OPHTHAL-MOLOGY 眼科 ganka	RADIOLOGY 放射線科 hōshasenka	ANESTHESI-OLOGY 麻酔科 masuika
DOCTOR 医者 isha	AMBULANCE 救急車 kyūkyūsha	HOSPITAL ROOM 病室 byōshitsu	PHARMACY 薬局 yakkyoku	OUTPATIENT DEPT. 外来 gairai
NURSE 看護師 kangoshi	CASHIER 会計 kaikei	RECEPTION DESK 受付 uketsuke	MEDICAL COSTS 医療費 iryōhi	CONSULTING HOURS 診療時間 shinryō jikan
PATIENT 患者 kanja	EMERGENCY ROOM 救急病院 kyūkyū byōin	WAITING ROOM 待合室 machiaishitsu	WHEELCHAIR 車いす kuruma isu	VISITING HOURS 面会時間 menkai jikan

NO ILL FEELING

I'm still not feeling well.	Aikawarazu yoku arimasen.	あいかわらずよくありません。
I feel a little better.	Sukoshi yoku narimashita.	少しよくなりました。
I feel much better.	Taihen yoku narimashita.	大変よくなりました。
Must I go to the hospital?	Nyūin shinakereba ikemasen ka?	入院しなければいけませんか。
Can I still travel?	Ryokō o tsuzukete mo ii desu ka?	旅行を続けてもいいですか。
How long do I have to take it easy?	Nan nichi kurai ansei ga hitsuyō desu ka?	何日くらい安静が必要ですか。
How long until I get better?	Dono kurai de yoku narimasu ka?	どのくらいでよくなりますか。

ESSENTIAL VERBS

to become sick
病気になる
byōki ni naru

to be injured
けがをする
kega o suru

to bleed
出血する
shukketsu suru

to break a bone
骨折する
kossetsu suru

to sprain
ねんざする
nenza suru

to get burned
やけどする
yakedo suru

to examine, to test
検査する
kensa suru

to take temperature
体温を計る
taion o hakaru

to take an x-ray
レントゲンをとる
rentogen o toru

to give an injection
注射をする
chūsha o suru

to operate
手術する
shujutsu suru

to be hospitalized
入院する
nyūin suru

to leave the hospital
退院する
taiin suru

to visit a patient
お見舞いに行く
o-mimai ni iku

to be pregnant
妊娠している
ninshin shite iru

to deliver a baby
出産する
shussan suru

to have an abortion
中絶する
chūzetsu suru

to miscarry
流産する
ryūzan suru

keisatsu
police

Problems
POLICE

Socially, male-dominated Japan may not be the modern woman's ideal place. But for safety on the street, Japan is nearly ideal, as crime rates are low and a woman can generally travel alone in most areas with little fear of attack or abuse. However, violent crime, while rare, does exist. Moreover, women need to exercise caution when walking alone at night. Some intoxicated Japanese males may become rude and sexually harass women on the street or on public transportation, and after dark it is always better to travel in groups and stick to well-lit streets with heavier foot traffic.

There is another uncomfortable, though not dangerous, place for a woman: the train. During rush hour, when they can take advantage of the inhuman way passengers are packed together, sad perverts called *chikan* grope women standing next to them. During rush hour, some subways and trains now have female-only cars to help address this problem.

The police have considerable powers, including detention of suspects for up to one month without charges. Like the ubiquitous police boxes, or *kōban*, police powers (and the obedient behavior of citizens) are a residue of samurai times, when a wrong word or act brought the unfavorable verdict of a swift sword.

In a low-crime place like Japan, the police spend most of their time patrolling on bicycles and giving directions. Should you need help, seek out the nearest *kōban* or police officer; s/he will go out of his way to help and many police have a smattering of English skills, especially in areas popular with foreign tourists.

156

EMERGENCIES

Help!	Tasukete!	助けて！
I'm lost.	Michi ni mayotte imasu.	道に迷っています。
Please help me.	Tasukete kudasai.	助けて下さい。
Come with me.	Issho ni kite kudasai.	一緒に来て下さい。
Where's the police box?	Kōban wa doko desu ka?	交番はどこですか。
How do I get there?	Dō yatte iku n'desu ka?	どうやって行くんですか。
Call the police, please.	Keisatsu o yonde kudasai.	警察を呼んで下さい。
Call a doctor, please.	Isha o yonde kudasai.	医者を呼んで下さい。
I must go to the hospital.	Byōin e ikanakute wa narimasen.	病院へ行かなくてはなりません。
Please call an ambulance.	Kyūkyūsha o yonde kudasai.	救急車を呼んで下さい。
Where is the lost-and-found?	Ishitsubutsu toriatsukaijo wa doko desu ka?	遺失物取扱所はどこですか。

POLICE QUERIES

If you've gone to the police with a problem, or if they've come to you with a problem, they may want to know a little more about you. Oblige.

Excuse me, what's written here?	Sumimasen ga koko wa nanto kaite arimasu ka?	すみませんがここは何と書いてありますか。
Excuse me, could you write it in roman letters?	Sumimasen ga rōmaji de kaite kudasai.	すみませんがローマ字で書いて下さい。
I need an interpreter.	Tsūyaku ga hitsuyō desu.	通訳が必要です。
Does somebody here speak English?	Dareka eigo o hanaseru hito wa imasu ka?	誰か英語を話せる人はいますか。

Do you have a passport?
パスポートはありますか。

Do you have money?
お金はありますか。

Do you have an ID card?
身分証明書はありますか。

How long are you staying in Japan?
日本にはどのくらいいるつもりですか。

Where did you come from?
どこから来ましたか。

Please come with me to the police box.
一緒に交番まで来て下さい。

157

LOST OR STOLEN

Excluding the danger presented by pickpockets who work places like airports, crowded trains, and busy shopping areas, money and belongings are relatively safe. A lost wallet or bag will usually turn up, and with all its contents intact.

Any traveler should always have photocopies of his passport, visa, and other important papers. Likewise, serial numbers are invaluable in retrieving lost (or, rarely, stolen) items like cameras and laptop computers. Keeping a card from your hotel in your bag will aid in getting it back to you. Should you require a police report in order to be reimbursed by your insurance company for lost or stolen items, you should be aware that it will be difficult to get one outside of the major cities. In any case, it'll be in Japanese.

I lost ~.	~ o nakushimashita.	～をなくしました。
I left ~ in a taxi/train/bus.	Takushii/Densha/Basu ni ~ o wasuremashita.	タクシー／電車／バスに～を忘れました。
My ~ was stolen.	~ o nusumaremashita.	～を盗まれました。
wallet	saifu	財布
cash	genkin	現金
passport	pasupōto	パスポート
driver's license	menkyoshō	免許証
ID card	mibun shōmeisho	身分証明書
camera	kamera	カメラ
glasses	megane	めがね
handbag	handobaggu	ハンドバッグ
package/luggage	nimotsu	荷物
suitcase	sūtsukēsu	スーツケース
watch	tokei	時計

Please write down your name, telephone number, and address in Japan.
この紙に名前、電話番号、住所を書いてください。

Please describe the item(s).
どういう物ですか。

PROBLEMS

There's a/an ~.	~ desu.	〜です。
fire	kaji	火事
accident	jiko	事故
traffic accident	kōtsū jiko	交通事故
crime	hanzai	犯罪
theft	nusumi	盗み
fraud, scam	sagi	詐欺
pickpocket	suri	すり
thief	dorobō	泥棒
Whom should I tell?	Dare ni shirasetara ii desu ka?	誰に知らせたらいいですか。

FIRE 火事 kaji	**ROAD ACCIDENT** 交通事故 kōtsū jiko	**CRIME** 犯罪 hanzai	**FRAUD, SCAM** 詐欺 sagi	**DETECTIVE** 刑事 keiji
FIRE TRUCK 消防車 shōbōsha	**AMBULANCE** 救急車 kyūkyūsha	**THEFT** 盗み nusumi	**POLICE** 警察 keisatsu	**POLICE STATION** 警察署 keisatsusho
FIRE STATION 消防署 shōbōsho	**INJURY** 怪我 kega	**PICKPOCKET** すり suri	**POLICE OFFICER** 警察官 keisatsukan	**POLICE BOX** 交番 kōban
NATIONALITY 国籍 kokuseki	**JUDGE** 裁判官 saibankan	**CRIMINAL** 犯人 hannin	**OFFENSE** 犯行 hankō	**EVIDENCE** 証拠 shōko
EMBASSY 大使館 taishikan	**LAWYER** 弁護士 bengoshi	**THIEF** 泥棒 dorobō	**GUILT** 有罪 yūzai	**PRISON, JAIL** 刑務所 keimusho
COURT OF LAW 裁判所 saibansho	**WITNESS** 証人 shōnin	**LEGAL ADVICE** 法律相談 hōritsu sōdan	**INNOCENCE** 無罪 muzai	**INSURANCE** 保険 hoken